SUPREMELY TINY ACTS

21st CENTURY ESSAYS

David Lazar and Patrick Madden, Series Editors

SUPREMELY TINY ACTS

A MEMOIR OF A DAY

Sonya Huber

MAD CREEK BOOKS, AN IMPRINT OF
THE OHIO STATE UNIVERSITY PRESS
COLUMBUS

Published by Mad Creek Books, an imprint of The Ohio State University Press.

Library of Congress Cataloging-in-Publication Data
Names: Huber, Sonya, 1971– author.
Title: Supremely tiny acts : a memoir of a day / Sonya Huber.
Description: Columbus : Mad Creek Books, an imprint of The Ohio State University
    Press, [2021] | Series: 21st century essays | Summary: "A book-length essay that
    details a mother's court appearance for civil disobedience in New York City in
    2019 and reflects on protest, privilege, and the role of everyday life in political
    change."—Provided by publisher.
Identifiers: LCCN 2021016482 | ISBN 9780814258040 (paperback) | ISBN 0814258042
    (paperback) | ISBN 9780814281536 (ebook) | ISBN 0814281532 (ebook)
Subjects: LCSH: Civil disobedience—New York (State)—New York—History—
    21st century. | Huber, Sonya, 1971—Political activity. | Climatic changes—New
    York (State)—New York. | Political activists—New York (State)—New York. |
    Motherhood—New York (State)—New York.
Classification: LCC JC328.3 .H83 2021 | DDC 303.6/1092 [B]—dc23
LC record available at https://lccn.loc.gov/2021016482

Cover design by Nathan Putens
Text design by Juliet Williams
Type set in Adobe Garamond Pro

I SLEPT LIKE SHIT, a feeling like chewing on tinfoil, sleep a thin battered substance. I knew the whole night that I had to get up early, and I absolutely had to go down to the city for court, and now I am nervous about it, nervous about how I've wedged this day together in a nonsensical stack of hours.

The Fitbit vibrates on my wrist, a concession to many years of waking to a jazzy five-note iPhone riff. Now when I hear that ringtone, cortisol soaks me in a car wash of images: white venetian blinds, Georgia heat, wake up to get the kid to daycare. The sound brings me back to a time when I was a divorcing then divorced single mom being slowly forced out of a tenure-track job because I'd been too mouthy about what they were doing to nontenured people. That was then, this is now, and I'm in Connecticut. I double tap on the black rectangular face of the Fitbit.

I say to my body, "I'm not going to jail." My body will not be talked down and has already achieved liftoff. I take deep breaths but then fuck up the rhythm and feel worse. Better just to leave my lungs alone and not micromanage.

I told students never to start a story with someone waking up in bed, but here I go and I'm not even a cockroach. I take out my earplugs, putty-colored foam nubs like the heads of little bald men.

I AM GOING TO COURT TODAY, November 19, 2019, because I was arrested on October 10 in a civil disobedience action in Times Square in New York, organized by the group Extinction Rebellion, to protest government inaction on climate change. A neon-green boat was hauled into the center of the intersection, and then people chained and glued themselves to it, and other people sat on the asphalt in a circle around the boat holding signs, and it lasted for a time span that felt like forever but I think it was only a half hour, followed by an hour of being handcuffed that also felt like forever, and then ten hours in jail. Extinction Rebellion started in London in 2018. The group did a lot of boat actions and took over bridges, but they did it with papier-mâché octopuses and fish costumes, and the demonstrations were so huge and playful and family friendly, had interesting visuals yet were saying things that were true and clear and serious about the threat facing us.

I first saw those actions on Twitter as XR spread to chapters all over the world, and then I researched XR and signed up for information, and then I saw the call for participation in the action. I'd wanted to get arrested for some of the protests against the immigration abuses at the border and was on a mailing list here in Connecticut for people battling court and ICE detention, but then I couldn't make the timing work with those trainings, though I would eventually get trained to do court accompaniment right before the pandemic. But I knew I was going to be arrested for something, I had to, because Trump's America was like living in an avalanche, and though I know it's bad to throw around facile comparisons to Hitler's Germany, I had been soaking in reading and thinking about my German relatives for decades, the question of how and at what point to be ready to throw my body somewhere where it might make a difference, as a German-American watching the dovetailing of chaos and racism and xenophobia and closing borders and corruption and abuse. There was no rescue in the fantasy of a return to normal, no "after" or reset button, no healing or past greatness, and this country would have to be forged into something new because hate had spread in a viral replication for so long. I knew that my privilege allowed me to get arrested and survive such a confrontation, and that privilege also obligated me to act because of the protections it afforded me.

I finally felt like I had my head above water enough to manage this. I'd never been arrested, though I'd planned for it once, during the first Gulf War, with legal support from some Quakers. I had a bunch of other opportunities but I didn't really understand how things worked, didn't get that if there was a demo there was usually legal support with bail money. I'd always opted out at the last minute because of vague fears about the money, which I didn't have, and I couldn't ask my Midwestern parents to rescue me when, at the time, they didn't support or were confused by what I was doing.

This morning the whole mobilization to get to court is worse than rushing to make an international flight, and I've been kind of weepy for a week—crying in my writing group, crying in the car. This fall semester has been a little over the top, with a trip out to Illinois for dad's emergency open-heart surgery in September. Add getting arrested into a semester—well, I'm often overly optimistic or just clueless about what might be too much. I cram whatever fits into the boxes of the calendar. And today I've got to make it back home after court in New York to take my son Ivan to get his driver's permit at 2 p.m. in Connecticut, so clearly I've scheduled things badly.

I find my glasses and get up in the dark, already imagining various calamities that might stop me from getting down to the physical courthouse in New York, because I'm a worst-case-scenario kind of woman. I go out into the dining room to take my purple and white thyroid pills because I have Hashimoto's disease and my thyroid is dissolving itself but it's not a big deal. My rheumatoid disease has been the real problem, because the pain is almost a physical substance that prevents me from moving in the world the way I imagine I should be able to. My pill container is stocked, four rows of pills, seven columns stacked with little plastic doors. Next to it, there's a square note on the dining room table I left for myself, on the golden veneer surface that is a little rippled and scratched, an amazing find from the Habitat for Humanity store in town, $50, still proud of it, replaced the very depressing $10 table I got from a junk place when we first moved up to Connecticut from Georgia, where Cliff had been unemployed and my salary was low and we'd had to borrow from everyone and take out a loan from my employer at my fancy new professor gig.

My square reminder note on the table says "Charger, water, grading" because without reminders and packing lists I am too distracted to remember basic stuff, and I don't know whether it is early mental fading or exhaustion. I feel like multi-tasking and mothering and worrying have done something to my brain, I'm forty-eight, and it's not so much that I can't think, but rather that my brain is tired. Which is why this re-creation was not written in a single draft, and which is why all credit to Karl Ove Knausgaard for claiming that six volumes of his autobiographical *My*

Struggle (yes, which I read, all of them, which is maybe why I'm a little cranky about it) came out of him in a text orgasm without an edit, but my writing has to come out in crumbs and messes that I glue together slowly because I am too exhausted and fragmented to be coherent from the get-go and that's okay, in fact I think the collage and also the conversation with one's self is really what's in it for me, the sense of being accompanied, of getting to know and not hate myself, the sense that a block of text is smarter than I am because it's a series of snapshots of me over time with all the dead bits pared away like the eyes of potatoes you edge out with the tip of a knife. It's me plus caffeine with all the clarity highlighted.

I'm taking your time with my real-life bullshit, and there's no excuse for it. So I should either apologize, or I should swing around my six-volume book-cock and assume my own brilliance, but there's no amount of coffee in the world that could get me to that level of confidence. So I'm going to assume I'm among friends. This day, November 19, 2019, isn't the best day or the worst day or anything, it is just a day that sticks in my head because of the chemistry of adrenaline, downtime, and notes made in a journal. But I have always liked the idea of watching the mind in the container of a day, because really one of my favorite books ever is Nicholson Baker's *The Mezzanine,* though that's a novel, and it's not even a whole day, but what I love about it is that the narrator rides escalators and buys shoelaces, and I know there's a complex beautiful structure inside it but really it's about the mind of a person having an amazingly normal web of thoughts, like those symphonies going on inside all of us all the time, beautiful invisible kaleidoscopes, and I always wanted to do that for real, to write that.

And then Ander Monson, an essayist and writing professor who likes gnomes and lives in the desert and who I once saw from a distance at a conference in Iowa and always thought was so cool because of his essays, did this thing where he asked a bunch of people to write about their days, all on June 21, 2018, and whatever happened that day was what you wrote about in a mini-essay, so it's like you paid attention as it happened and kept notes, and then he published them on his website. When I did my essay, there was a combination of randomness and connection, and yes, it's kind of Heisenberg-uncertainty-principle artificial because you're watching the experiment and so you're sort of changing it by watching, but sort of not because you still have to live your life, and the current of hours ends up overriding your plans, as life does. On the day we were supposed to write, I had received an email about a bad result from a liver-function blood test, and then I went to the grocery store with my son, and those things got caught in the net of words like they never would normally, and then there was also the sense that other people, hundreds of them, were making these documents too, and that was lovely, part of this yearning I think we have to get to the real, to catch the facts we have, to hold on to what we see, induction, in this time where lies are currency and power and are endangering us all.

But I did not get up today intending to write about it. Instead I am surging with a focus to check the boxes, get things done, as an overfocused good-girl don't-be-late I'm-scared-of-being-in-trouble and scared-of-the-Man, but then I notice my thoughts more during the downtime because as a nervous Buddhist, that is what I do to not panic quite so often.

And this documentation is not about heroism, because getting arrested was selfish, in a way. I'm extremely lucky and privileged that I can do it safely, and it was a chance for one day to live in alignment with values or ethics, which are being blasted out of us by living in the sandstorm of klepto-fascism. But what I mean is that every day is draining because the hours are made up of attempts to keep functioning and keep a job and do normal things and microwave mozzarella sticks for one's teenage son (actually don't microwave, these should go in the toaster oven, trust me) and so every day dealing with the mundane is a stark wrongness, a sign that we are all more split inside, that we have to dissociate or compartmentalize, but I don't think people are numb or tuning out, we're just all divided in several pieces and we know we should constantly be setting things on fire so we are trying to figure out what constitutes ethical action. In five months, the next wave of Black Lives Matter actions will swell up in the midst of the COVID-19 pandemic, and I will get sick and stay sick for six months and will become what they will call a long hauler, and the opportunities to protest will multiply along with the tornado of wrongs as my body is busy remaking itself around a virus.

But this is the before-time, and this get-arrested-by-choice was on some level a chance to check a box or know that I did something, even though this was not the only thing I did, but who's counting? I'm counting. Always. And I'm desperate to find a way to sleep at night, but how do any of us sleep? Part of what's hard these days is that even these formerly meaningful acts seem meaningless or puny in the face of imminent planetary and human destruction. And my son gets that. He asked me after court what I was going to do about global warming and I said, "Well I just went to jail last month," and he looked at me deadpan and asked, "Well, did that work?" He has a point. But then again, this is faith for me, the faith that people who care about making the world better have to add their supremely tiny acts together, and if you can function in that constant impossibility of your tiny actions, then you can contribute grains of sand that might stop the engine of doom.

TO PREPARE FOR THE ACTION in October I had to go to a half-day training in New York City on a Sunday in September, so I drove down from Connecticut and paid about $30 to park in a parking garage underneath a church, near some university, maybe Columbia. It was a large old stone church where all kinds of political meetings were happening, and I took the elevator up and followed signs along stone carved hallways. About fifty of us filed in with our coffees and claimed chairs in a gym with a stage, and presenters went through the XR philosophies projected onto a screen, and there was no ice-breaker bullshit. I was impressed at the level of organization, and the emphasis on connecting with the emotional effects of living under the threat of climate change, and on the simplicity of the message and the demands, the first of which is just "Tell the Truth," as in tell the truth about climate change. And any question about "how do we fix this" and "how do we feel about which solutions will work and how do we remake the world" are deferred to the idea of citizens' assemblies. The basic idea—very appealing and practical—is that having a complete program for a new society is a luxury we don't have time for, and whoever actually gets near that situation will figure out. I love that: trust the future to work itself out. In XR there's a lot of street theater, including a Red Brigade that wears red gowns and head coverings and face paint, and even a crew of volunteer therapists. I'm impressed at the ways that the group is trying to sustain itself and its people because this stuff can get draining. Even confrontations with other well-meaning activists can eat you alive.

The UK group has three clear demands, and the US group added a fourth, which is "We demand a just transition that prioritizes the most vulnerable people and indigenous sovereignty; establishes reparations and remediation led by and for Black people, Indigenous people, people of color and poor communities for years of environmental injustice, establishes legal rights for ecosystems to thrive and regenerate in perpetuity, and repairs the effects of ongoing ecocide to prevent extinction of human and all species, in order to maintain a livable, just planet for all." I liked that the US group had stepped up with that, which must have taken lots of discussion. But still the group is mostly white, which I think is partially because of structure and the time commitments required and partially because of activist cultures in the environmental movement. Later, next spring, the group will use its network in support of the Black Lives Matter protests. In the training we did small setups of potential "soft-blocks" where you form a human shield by linking elbows with people on each side of you and clasping your hands together, one over and under, in two interlocking C shapes. They didn't tell us what we were actually going to do, because they had to keep it a secret, and we would know right before the action.

What I told my friends afterward was that I didn't feel any major red flags from the organization, although I'm sure they are there. I've been in a bunch of organizations and seen all kinds of dysfunction: from overly authoritarian to overly disorganized, so many demands from small organizations in no place to win any of them. I have watched major socialist organizations get derailed with fierce hours-long debates about their position on what was happening to the trade unionists in Ecuador, and yes it was important to issue a statement in support but then came the yelling and the quoting of Gramsci versus Trotsky and references to the various Internationals, which were gatherings of communists and socialists that produced different viewpoints and disagreements over the last century. I have been involved in this for straight-up thirty years and I still don't get it, because my mind tends toward the practical, like what are we doing here and now, and I still think it's wrong to not build enough resilience into an organization to not split over random debates. I know there's some old white Maoist somewhere who'd want to deck me for that, and I can say that because once, in a recruitment meeting for a secret Maoist organization in some living room in New York, a Maoist with bad teeth (cynically I wonder if he neglected his teeth on purpose as a statement in solidarity with the global working class) scoffed at something I'd said and called me "little girl" and I was at least twenty-five. So that's an example of a red flag, and not the good kind.

OCTOBER 10, THE DAY of the action where I got arrested, was sunny and unseasonably warm. I had left the house before dawn with my "embed's" cell phone number on my arm in permanent marker. He was the coordinator of our small group, had been arrested before, and this time was there to hold our phones and see us off and then wait for us outside until we got let out of jail. Since I'm a stress-case in general I was grateful for how much support the group provided. I arrived like I was going off to sleep in the streets for two weeks: tights under my jeans because it was supposed to rain, a raincoat, a pad in my underwear because I didn't know how long this whole thing was supposed to go on, and what would you do if you had to pee? I didn't want a UTI on top of everything. I had a small packet of Advil and several protein bars jammed in my bra.

We gathered in Bryant Park, the sun streaming golden from behind a few clouds, and we signed in near some tables and a newspaper kiosk and tried to be inconspicuous. A woman named R. who I recognized from the training had also showed up early, and we started chatting, both short, dark-haired, nervous but shy in a way that made us seem bitter but really came from anxiety. We both confessed that we'd worn adult diaper pads and we both started laughing like crazy because that's who we were: overprepared fierce little women who would tell that kind of thing to a fellow stranger about to get arrested.

Eventually as more of us gathered, we were broken up into groups and given separate jobs. A guy came and described what we were actually going to do, and then another person came to sit at our table under the trees. I recognized her as one of the coordinators from the training. She slapped down a rough pencil sketch of the intersection on the cement table, then drew a circle with her finger to show the corner of the intersection where we were going to gather. She then dragged her finger toward the intersection, showing us where the boat would come through traffic, and then on what signal we were supposed to go out into the intersection to make a human ring around the boat, clasping hands and sitting down.

Then our embed came with two big plastic bags, and he pulled out sheaves of rolled fabric flags, setting each stack on the cement table. We were to each take a flag to represent places endangered by rising seas. As I pulled out the flag of Malawi, a sleepy and tall white boy with long arms and legs said "Wait!" and he asked what it meant that a crew of mostly white and privileged American people were holding the signs of disappearing coastal nations from the Global South. Was it better to have the flags, or not hold them, not claim that we represented the world? Wasn't that bad, optically? Or was it worse to not express solidarity? We landed on the fact that it was better to mention the world, to get beyond us and our little white lives. On the flag of Malawi, someone had neatly written in permanent marker the number of deaths caused by a catastrophic storm. I rolled up the flag into my sleeve, checked my watch, looked around. Finally someone said it was time to go, and we rushed, excited, nervous, hurrying, glancing, *Is this the right way?* Intersection crosswalk, looking forward and back at each other along the sidewalk as if we were all new friends, as if we were much younger, as if this were grade school or camp, the kind of feeling from childhood where a group of complete strangers suddenly have a secret and a common purpose.

We got to Times Square and waited on a street corner, and we'd been told to spread out and not gather in groups or be obvious. I exchanged a few sentences with a woman I hadn't seen before who told me she was part of the film crew, and she pointed to where the boat would arrive. Then she got a text and said they were near. The small truck towing a boat appeared in traffic, inching slowly. In my head I think I had expected a huge clipper ship with tall masts, some kind of direct-action ghost pirate ship, which I realized was hilarious as soon as I saw the small motorboat. The truck pulled it through the intersection with traffic

but then stopped, and someone told us *Yes—Now* and we ran
out into the intersection in Times Square in a dream-like surge
beneath the flashing rectangles of flat splashy red-white-pink-
yellow ads and curving surfaces, and the blue and silvery flashes
seemed to be cheering us on.

We circled the boat, rushing to grab the hands of people next
to us, because we were the first barrier. More people arrived and
our circle thickened and we distributed ourselves, our hands
filled with flags, and in the shuffling I ended up at the back of
the boat. On a signal we all sat down, and each separate team did
their choreographed role. People standing on each corner strung
lengths of orange plastic snow fencing temporarily across all the
crosswalks to block traffic in all directions while we set up. The
chains clanked on the boat and people clambered behind us and
onto it and underneath it, and we looked over our shoulders to
check the progress of the boat as horns honked, and we grabbed
each other's hands and faced outward like ring around the rosy
in reverse, and there were more clanks and rattles of chains as
people began attaching themselves to the boat, and I think the
wheels were removed from the trailer to make it harder to move
the boat. Each person followed the action plan they'd been given,
and there were people behind us standing on the boat, chained
under the boat, with their hands glued to the boat, to make the
removal process longer, to make the action more impactful, and
the police would have to use some kind of nail polish remover
to dissolve the glue, and they would have to cut the chains, and
this would also allow longer for media coverage and for conversations in the street about the action. The sheer beauty of the
action unfolded like origami.

Photos of me from the event are hilarious: I look like a daunted child, eyes wide and mouth a serious little line. I held a corner of the flag of Malawi and chanted along with everyone as I sat there on the asphalt. It was mostly impossible not to stare at the wall of pedestrians, the panorama of people arrayed on the crosswalks and all around us, almost like a kind of woven human nest, layered and thick with faces and hands and expressions and chanting and signs, wrapping around us. They were holding iPhones, looking at us with delight, yelling with joy, taking pictures, chanting, giving us thumbs-up, a wall of people and noise between us and the stretching glass and concrete of the building, the noise behind us and around us, filling the sky above us like a column. Then the setup people rolled away the orange fencing they had strewn and stretched across the roadways.

A guy with a shaggy Afro and squarish glasses, wearing a worn gray canvas jacket with a lot of pockets, held a bullhorn and led chants, facing us and turning also, trying to get the crowd around us involved in the chants, and I liked the way he smiled with sly joy as he chanted that we weren't going to stay silent near the end of the world, and next to him a serious guy with a shorn head stood with a big tray of equipment slung from a belt and held a television camera, and another person held a long microphone, all I could see were his arms with the boom mike wavering and nudging like the nose of an animal. We chanted, "The seas are rising, and so are we!"

In the crowd of pedestrians a guy nearest me held up his phone and filmed, and the sheer happiness on his face was like we had given him the best present ever. He couldn't stop laughing, his eyes and mouth wide, and looking at other people near him, as if to say, "Can you believe this?" And then there were

girls chewing gum and filming, and their phones with lavender
and pink cases and those pop-socket buttons and manicured
pastel nails, and they sort of floated by and disappeared like a
mirage. I wasn't prepared for how overjoyed people would be to
see us, that they would look almost *relieved* to see traffic stop in
Times Square because this, after all, was necessary. This was all
interesting and overwhelming because we'd been prepped in our
action training to deal with angry pedestrians and tourists, people upset to be interrupted in the middle of their day, and I get
that. Maybe someone would be late to an important and serious
doctor's appointment, and that was a scary thing in and of itself
to contemplate—that we were stopping not only tourists but
also people with major things to do, like their own court dates or
tearful lunch meetings. So maybe that was happening, silently, in
the lines of cars radiating outward from the intersection, people
behind wheels swearing and looking at watches and craning their
necks above the steering wheel, like you do when you're in a long
jam, like if only you could *see* the problem then you'd feel better. In our action training, we were advised to be empathetic and
de-escalate, to apologize and say this was necessary and it would
end. But I hadn't counted on the joy.

Orange cardboard circles with holes cut in the middle were
painted like life preservers, and they were passed around, but it
turned out that we had too many things to hold, so they were
scattered around the boat on the pavement along with strips of
garbage bag or rubber that I think were supposed to be seaweed,
and then later after the police arrived, someone crouch-ran and
picked them up. TV cameras appeared from nowhere, panning
around us, and a reporter asked me a question, held a camera
and a microphone, and I don't even know what I said but I'm

sure it wasn't very stirring. I treated it as a pop quiz and was stiff and scared like I was going to give the wrong answer. It was good that I was on one end of the boat by happenstance, the back of the boat, and the most photo-ready picture of the event was from the side of the boat to my left, where you could see the Extinction Rebellion logo and the people glued to the mast and chanting and being awesome in a way that I didn't have in me, because I hadn't been arrested before. I was sitting on the pavement on top of my raincoat. And then someone gave me yet another little flag on a stick to hold, I don't even remember what it was, so I was holding a lot of things. We ended up making a barrier with the flags so that they could be visible, and I was holding one corner of the Malawi flag and the other corner was being held by an older guy with a beard named Sean. On my other side was R., and we were all part of the circle of about fifty in the human barrier.

I don't remember how long it took for the police to arrive, but it was a special unit that apparently deals both with terrorism and with demonstrators. Could that be right? I might have gotten that wrong. To them of course this was not impressive, just a day at work. They gathered like you see on murder shows, hanging around in clumps that look like a dangerous cocktail party, chatting and not really doing anything, looking at what they could see with their police-eyes about what had to happen to clear away this blockage. They seemed to be waiting for something or someone else to arrive, in no hurry to do anything at all. Then a more important police guy arrived, looking off into the distance, and you could tell by who clumped together that there were various levels of authority and the highest people didn't have to wear a uniform. There were gobs of police and all of them seemed to be on their phones or maybe trying to look like police officers. Is there such a thing as a cop with imposter syndrome?

A police officer hauled out a black portable speaker and set it very near me in front of a parked car at the street corner near the base of a traffic light. It faced toward us and a very loud electric voice chanted over and over that we'd be arrested if we didn't move out of the street, a recorded message they must have had to use many times, at a deafening volume that made everything feel more on edge. The photo of me might have been taken after that noise started, because it was challenging to keep one's thoughts together over that racket; it was hard to think. Then the police were holding stacks of white plastic handcuffs like big double-looped zip ties. They started telling us one by one to get up, and they worked in groups of four or five, but they started from the other side of the boat. We were told in our training not to resist arrest, that going limp was going to lead to higher charges and that wasn't part of the strategy for growing this movement.

I'VE BEEN LIVING AS IF my actions are a note in a bottle to a future that might not exist, Schrödinger's Tomorrow, and I've been in that headspace my whole life, the hovering discomfort beginning in the 1980s when I was 8 or 9 and first understood the Cold War, writing to President Reagan to try to convince him that if there were a nuclear war he would also not have jelly beans anymore, a candy-based case for saving humanity, and in response months later I got a formatted newsletter from the White House about kids and politics that was complete bullshit, and I knew that even then, and I threw it away. I wasn't precious enough to save any of those records of my early activism because that was not the kind of family I was from, not the kind that recognized itself in resistance, and my anger at society was a furtive secret.

That was before I started making hand-drawn T-shirts with quotes about the dangers of nuclear war, copying quotes from a library book onto a Hanes shirt from Kmart with toothpicks dipped in fabric paint, and then I wore those under loose flannels to school at a time when I think I was the only political-shirt-wearing person in a place where my graduating class alone was over 700 people. I went to a farm-town high school in Illinois, a massive and pretty authoritarian place south of Chicago without a student newspaper known as having the best discipline in the state, not Evanston at all. At some point after I stopped curling my hair with a curling iron in the late 1980s style, someone carved "LESBO" in the dark green paint of my locker in the hallway near the band room, even though I had a boyfriend on the soccer team. I kept that to myself. I was always afraid about doing my tiny things, leaving hand-drawn flyers in the grocery store about the dangers of dioxin bleach in the paper products and chlorofluorocarbons, but I always did them anyway, compulsed as only a Catholic girl raised on visions of saintly bodily sacrifice can be, like Saint Lucy holding her eyeballs on a platter, the wounds of stigmata as honor, raised that suffering equals love and that justice requires a blood sacrifice. Well, it often does.

In 1988, because of where I grew up and how, I didn't know there were stores where you could buy T-shirts with slogans about social change. I got on a mailing list after I joined Amnesty International and eventually subscribed to the *Utne Reader* and then I found in the classified ads places like Northern Sun based in Minneapolis that had a catalog you could send away for and then I bought my first T-shirts that someone else had screen-printed with slogans.

This just kept going on and off for decades, during which time I acquired many printed cotton T-shirts that say things like "I Walked the Line with Local 169" and "Fuck Fascism" and "Not Today, Patriarchy," to which my husband Cliff always responds, *How about tomorrow?*

There is an engine in me that makes me speak up that is equal to my fear of speaking up. I took Kant and Christ very seriously, even though I just recently learned Kant is some kind of racist and he's been rolling around in my head for thirty years. What can we do against the roaring train of destruction? In grad school I researched and wrote the story of my German socialist grandfather. After growing up in a small Republican town in Illinois and wanting activist mentors, it turned out I had one but I'd never met him or really been told anything about him, and my mom didn't really even know much because she left home at sixteen. I researched and interviewed and dug and stitched the story together and wrote a book to explain to my mother what her father's life meant. And then I had something more to measure myself against, but I also had someone half-imaged to talk to, to understand the world, to whisper the answers I never got. The comforting fiction that people tell themselves, that "if it were the Nazi era I'd speak out," like hell you would, this is another test right now: democracy in flames. It's nice to get arrested and show up but I know the really hard thing is organizing these actions and making plans for actions that are necessary and meaningful. What I'm doing is okay. I'm mindful of my body, my energy level, forty-eight and usually in pain, my limitations and what I can give, yet always trying to find a little bit more, working the line between what I can do and what I can't. Cliff looked at me with alarm and both Cliff and Ivan were worried when I told them I wanted to be arrested and they looked at each other as if to say, *OK, this is what mom does,* and then after I got through it, I think they were proud. I am always pushing the edges.

SO HERE WE ARE and I'm headed to court and I haven't even had my first swallow of coffee.

I pour coffee with chicory and mix it with Hershey's cocoa powder in a thermos, which is my latest coffee concoction to distract myself from the fact that I gave up dairy as a way to reduce inflammation because of rheumatoid arthritis. I don't even know how many years it's been now, at least seven without dairy and gluten, and I've tried every goddamn thing in my coffee in every mixture to replicate the simple joy of half and half. As I'm stirring, a text on the blue-colored secure Signal app pops up on my phone from a person in our court group who wants to read a long statement in court today about global warming and urges everyone to make long speeches, which would make our day in court endless.

I get it. In some ways this was part of the point of our action, to register somewhere in the grinding machine that we are not okay with dying like this, that we are not okay with killing millions, that we demand to be heard. Yet muscles clench in my heart and gut because—dammit, I've got shit to do, what will happen if our case gets continued? I had to cancel classes today, and it is a privilege to have a flexible schedule, but clearing a day was a lot and I can't keep doing it. The "flexibility" of the schedule is balanced with a careening series of days and blocks of meetings and events and emails and assignments at such a pace that it's usually summer or Christmas by the time I realize my car needs an oil change and all the AA batteries have exploded in the kitchen junk drawer months ago.

I let myself do this, get arrested, because I finally got all the promotions they can give me, so I felt safer doing something that was outside my comfort zone. Should I text back and say something? *The moms are such a drag,* I can hear the young'uns say, those twenty-something white boys so on fire and yet in a way so bad at listening and most intent on telling us what it means to be a revolutionary. Still they are so much better than the boys in the 1990s, but now some of those boys have evolved. Some of these guys understand gender politics in a way my crew didn't.

There was one young man in our second XR civil disobedience training who tried to talk to me and was so beautiful and maybe nineteen or maybe in his twenties, and I thought he was high but it turned out was just incredibly beautiful and peaceful, an actor, and he was in my affinity group, and he was the one who wanted to look at all the flags we were given to hold in the park and to think about the racial dynamics, and good for him for caring. Our affinity group had formed at the second meeting right before the action in a cool community space somewhere in New York, a café on a leafy green street with brick buildings in a light rain, with images of revolutionaries painted in murals on the walls.

As I'm drinking my coffee, another text shows up that says "I need to get done by noon to get my kid from school in upstate New York at 3" and she (I assume it is a she) doesn't apologize, and I let out a whoosh of air. Someone said it, with no guilt or angst or self-deprecation, to the younger boys to alert them to the fact that some of us have things to do every hour we're awake.

I start to break apart a gluten-free bagel (Trader Joe's and surprisingly fantastic) and put it in the toaster, thinking about parents in social movements and how you're torn, always torn—and you're doing it for your kids but then you're away from them, distracted. Grace Paley, Tillie Olsen, those writer-activist moms. Also my grandfather, whose political work meant he was always away from his family. Tillie Olsen wrote *Silences* and I don't know if anyone reads that book anymore, but she was active in labor stuff in the 1930s in San Francisco and wrote about a life spent working and caring for kids instead of writing. Her book is very precious to me. I found it by accident in a box of free books on someone's lawn, I think, in Somerville, Massachusetts, where I lived after college in the 1990s, and I realized afterward how important she was to the wider world of activists. I think a lot, have thought a lot, about what it means to be truly inclusive of families in activist work, which has been one of the big puzzles of my life—how I had to pull back when my son Ivan was tiny, versus the idea that you shouldn't have had kids because the world is ending, or sure, the random abstract idea of bringing your kids to every action and meeting, which I tried to do until I found myself with my boob out breastfeeding an infant in the middle of a meeting at a plumber's union local in Columbus, Ohio, in a snowstorm. Then there's the fact that I'm not an endless resource, and I needed money and had limited time and energy. And yet I got frustrated, too, at people who would say, "Raising my kids is my activism." In a way I get it, but in another way, come on— there's time to do more than parenting, even if it's chopped up into quick bursts, and even if I couldn't be an organizer like I once was, but then again I only had one kid.

So as I stir my coffee, I weigh whether to chime in on the text chain that I'm in the same situation, and I consider how I would phrase a text. I really don't want to mess up Ivan's driving permit test, which matters a lot to him, but I don't want to get into a text war among activists. On some level I'm afraid of everyone, which is hilarious considering the fact that my face has been on the news for screaming myself hoarse at demonstrations, how I believe so much in group action but individually I'm kind of a weenie. Maybe this is how it should be, because we give each other courage.

Don't say anything. I'm pretty vocal, but then I always have a kickback of shame afterward, shame at drawing attention to myself, of people shaking their heads at me and thinking I'm a bitch, thinking that I think I'm right, being wrong. (As if having opinions is a crime, and not knowing is an equal crime. But that's deep in me.) I don't text my fear about the courthouse schedule and speeches, and I feel good for being quiet, that virtuous feeling that people must have that impels them to tune out from politics.

I still regret chiming in during a local debate on Facebook a few years ago about a curriculum controversy. The junior high administration proposed to remove advanced classes to end "tracking," or sorting kids into classes based on skill level, which often ends up reinforcing racial and class segregation. I asked in a parents' group why the administration would propose such a huge change but then do a shortcut: give parents only a week at the very end of the school year before a rushed board vote. I had been invited to a daytime focus group to learn about it, but no parents who worked could attend.

I voice my opinion a lot, but in this case I wasn't sure about my position, confused about what the change would require in terms of teachers' labor, and somehow the whole debate was stressful because it was so personal. School was life to me, and my heart thrummed with a kind of retrospective panic. In the Facebook debate I was told that the right social justice position today is against tracking and toward putting all the kids in the same classes, which sounds like going back to what my teachers were doing when I was in grade school in the 1970s, running between groups and giving multiple assignments to multiple work groups. And that's fine, but I searched for things to read about it and couldn't find articles or essays beyond "tracking is bad," and I wanted more detailed information about what it would be replaced with.

As a kid in junior high, I had many non-tracked classes in things I wasn't great at, as a chattering disruption in science classes. But I also had a pull-out class a few times a week in our Illinois farm-town fifth and sixth grade that was my oxygen. Ten or eleven of us sat on the carpet and read a story by Kurt Vonnegut, I think, in a special paperback filled with really weird stories, and we got an assignment to build a city of the future with a dome we spray-painted silver, in a school day where creativity was almost invisible. It was a treasure to be with the kids who everyone called the nerds, where it turned out that the awkward and distracting parts of my brain were useful. I worry for the nerdy writer girls who need that lifeline, that momentary encouragement and protection, and as someone from nowhere, from a working-class background transitioning to middle class, the first girl who ever went to college on either side of my family who did not have to join a convent to do so, I feel like those pull-out moments to protect creativity were a fulcrum for my whole life and what I thought I could be. I have carried them with me in my heart.

For the rest of the week, we were all in one classroom with work groups with different levels, in a hazy blur of worksheets and dullness. While listening to kids getting yelled at in the background, I hid Stephen King novels in my lap, *Firestarter*, and dreamt of flames. I raced through worksheets and then made clay animals and played with them on the metal lip of my desk shelf. I wish we were in a place and time where we could add things to school, more teachers and smaller class sizes, more art. Anything less is a bureaucratic game of pretend, a shell game of shuffling budget deficits from one hand to the other. Can schools really make up for the racism of society when zip codes are so segregated? I mean sure it is fine to try, but don't overpromise that there's a simple fix. And now the US is a devolving country, choosing in the midst of its wealth to burn its own future.

I'm glad Ivan will be out of public school in a few years. It's all been overwhelming, the forms that have to get signed, the physical that's always missing, the volunteering and teacher appreciation and valentines and transitions and registration and the urgent rush of due dates, and I compare myself to the "involved" moms and hide because I feel so inadequate. My son is a sophomore in high school and I have never been to a PTA meeting because I'm awful, I guess, it's just that I've never done well in groups of moms, like they are so normal and everything that comes out of my mouth is weird. Work is overwhelming enough as it is, plus writing, which is the time I suppose I steal from mothering.

I was very much a nerd but also kind of fear-driven, eagerly diving into any task, starving for structure and direction from the vague sadness in my head. I've had to see and accept how different my son is from me, how he doesn't fearfully cling to school and is part of the culture where swag comes from just being chill and doing the minimum amount of work. Is that like a biological thing with teenage boys? Nerd girls like me were so eager to please, so constantly edited and criticized, but I guess all kids do that to each other. He's been teased out of earnestness. I worry that I don't push him enough with his schoolwork, or maybe it's okay that I nudge rather than storm.

I don't take him to as many social justice events as I used to, hardly any now, because he doesn't seem interested or maybe it seems scary based on something I inadvertently said to him long ago that I have forgotten. I carried him as an infant in a front carrier on my chest to a loud Justice for Janitors demo in Columbus, Ohio, shaking beans in a soda can, maybe it was too loud for his little ears, and there's no way he could remember. Thinking about my choices and options, a montage of fantasies of ideal parents flits across my brain, hippies who read Shakespeare to their child in utero, and I wonder if I am even a good mom at all.

He's stubborn, my boy, and he knows his own mind, and maybe I lectured him too much about social justice stuff and now he kind of tunes me out. But in another way I know that the world is overwhelming and he's sensitive and he's scared, too, about the world ending.

All this flits by my mind in the two seconds that I skim the texts. Instead I stir my coffee with a low hum of anxiety about whether the schedule will work at all today. I have made a Plan B that my husband Cliff will come home early to take Ivan to the Hamden DMV north of New Haven if court takes too long and the schedule doesn't *klapp*. (The German verb is *es klappt*, which means everything sort of dovetails nicely, and sometimes there's a nice German verb that just works better than the English.)

I chew the toasted bagel with butter even though I'm mostly dairy free because fuck it the world is ending. I put a weird tan-colored protein drink in my bag, along with a bunch of protein bars, as if protein is what I need for sitting on public transportation all day, and I pack a folder of essays to grade, a printout of a talk on chronic pain I'm supposed to give on a webinar next Tuesday, and a printout draft of an article I agreed to write in three days, which is ridiculous but I'd kind of written about it before plus there was the ego thing of wanting to be in this particular publication, and anyway it was all based on the same pain stuff, which I know how to talk about through practice. I am so nervous about the webinar, like I am about all public things, yet I know that if I plan too closely it turns out worse, just like teaching. It's hard to trust that within me there's something good and amorphous that blooms in the moment, that my brain in the very very alive moment—the now—makes leaps that resonate, that I can say things off the cuff from the basis of knowledge, feeling the fingerprint, the terrain of living with others rather than trying to overcontrol.

My tendency is to plan things and make lists, to clutch a plan yet fear its requirements in the face of the chaos of the world. Plans and to-do lists are so essential to pulling me out of depression and fear, and once I started making epic to-do lists and combining that with the question of "What's the next right thing?" from Al-Anon (support group for friends and family of alcoholics and addicts) plus the list of three things each day toward your creative dream from Julia Cameron's *The Artist's Way*—yes, this is my lineage and I'm proud of it, it's middle-brow and accessible and it saved me—then everything started unfolding in my life, because that was the way I gained tiny, tiny courage to want things. Each item on my to-do list was a dare and a horrible confrontation with myself, made from the safety of my desk with a pen. Let's see if she can do this. Let's do this. Then the rule-following good-girl looked at the list and felt like I had to obey or it would be a sin, except the goals were things I wanted. I snuck into myself by using all the tools of repression against that shell.

Then also when I was in my twenties after college in Minnesota, I ended up moving to Boston and working at a bookstore in Harvard Square with a basement filled with used books, and I would go down with my employee discount and just buy the whole stack of writing guides at once. That was really my homemade MFA prep, or at least my orientation to what it meant to be a writer, because I'd always wanted to be a writer before I decided that wasn't doing enough for the world and plus anyway I had to work and so I went into direct care in social work in a teen residential center and had no idea it was possible to go to grad school without being rich. Also the guy who taught the Intro to Shakespeare undergrad class scared me and wanted to have a meeting with me in his office where our knees touched, and I had to explain why I wrote a short story for an academic paper assignment because I was difficult and I couldn't breathe and did things based on whether they provoked panic attacks, so I couldn't be an English major, so I was a sociology major instead.

So anyway, in the bookstore's basement I scooped up stacks of used books and happened upon sheer gold: John Gardner, Anne Lamott's *Bird by Bird,* Brenda Ueland's *If You Want to Write.* I found friends. I found Julia Cameron and Annie Dillard's *The Writing Life,* where she says, "A schedule is a net for catching days." I typed out that quote and taped it in a journal. And I did my three things a day for my writing, journaling and writing poems and sending them to tiny magazines and writing a bad novel on the subway, and with my slow work, I began to train myself to be a writer.

Also I found that structure and lists were magical for me to protect writing from the grinding engines of activism and work, how lists have let me focus, because as my husband says I'm a source of good chaos. I'm constantly living in the tangent. So I cling to schedules, write out lesson plans, but then if I go into the classroom and try to just do the things like a checklist, the class flattens, there's no air. You have to respond to the joyful opportunities that emerge, you have to pause and really really really learn to watch what arises and use that energy. As an organizer I did not learn that lesson, I was young, so I went into meetings without any trust in the energy of the universe. It always felt like chaos I was supposed to manage, but I felt like I was doing it badly.

I take another swig of coffee and I put on blue eyeliner and mascara, making myself face outward. I have come into this idea in my forties, based on watching my daily experience, that I'm treated more kindly when I wear makeup, and am less invisible, because sexism, and I am in this decade a little less terrified of any kind of attention from men because it's less frequent and less overwhelming. I pull on a ribbed gray-black mottled turtleneck with sleeves that are sort of stretched out and shapeless. I am dressing like a mom, conforming to the picture of being a woman, playing that smiley accommodating long-haired woman, and I have a mask that is charming to the extent that I can be. I can use a lot of my energy being noticed and sparkly and saying always, *Sure, I'm flexible.* Such a vice, such a habit. I put on dangly earrings, and yet I suppose this is also me, or a version that I like. Not every mom loves bright blue liquid eyeliner in swoops.

I slip on my black leather boots, laceless, like the laceless shoes we were warned in the civil disobedience training to wear to jail, otherwise the police would take the laces. Like the slip-on brown boots, I think people call them Chelsea boots now, that I used to have. Gonzo our awesome wild now-dead dog ate one from my old pair when we lived in Georgia. Gonzo the maybe-Australian shepherd, and the boots were from Australia where my mom's brother moved to escape their difficult family life in Germany after their mom died. My mom hunted her brother down decades later using a private investigator, but then he died of cancer before she got to see him. But we visited after he died to meet his family. Anyway Gonzo had flowing wings on her legs like Farrah Fawcett's swoops, that dog had excellent choice in literature, she ate Denis Johnson's *Tree of Smoke* (didn't read that one, it was Cliff's, who was my new boyfriend then after my messy divorce) and Salman Rushdie's *The Satanic Verses* in my office. Such a good girl, carrying pinecones like prizes in the Georgia heat. Gonzo was a stray my ex-husband found and brought home as a puppy, where she slept on the skateboard ramp he built in the driveway, and she dug pits that reached under the rental house's foundation in the sandy soil of Low-country Georgia.

I KEEP AN EYE on the time, the blue light of the early morning outside, my thermos of coffee, and what jacket do I wear? It's so cold out. I'm overthinking this. I want something warm but not bulky that I have to lug around and drop and that will make me all sweaty. I put on a wine-colored ski jacket from Costco but am quickly too hot. I look through the coat closet and take out a thin wool jacket that I bought in a discount place before Ivan was born while I was working at the alternative weekly news-paper in Columbus, where I was always pitching nerdy stories about regional planning. I snap the gray jacket that's green on the inside, and it's more snug over my boobs than it used to be. I stuff a black hat (weird thing, floppy, from some thrift store, and it always kind of looks like a cake on my head) and leather gloves (I used them for yard work, why did I do that, they're black and nice) into my bag, forgetting a scarf.

I grab the jangle of keys, with the misfit keychains of Lego Chewbacca torso with no hands, Lego Wonder Woman with her face rubbed off by the contact with the keys, and the plastic leaf with the Buddhist "This is it" script. I start the dirty black van in the cold, turn on the lights, pull back, away from our small house covered in yellow siding across the street from a Superfund site that we didn't know was a Superfund site when we bought it eight years ago. Now they're finally cleaning up the PCBs from the asbestos brake pads they made in that plant, but basically our whole industrial town is contaminated, and just as the EPA was starting with the project Trump was elected and then we were all freaking out at a community meeting and asking the EPA people standing at the front of the room if the EPA would even exist in two weeks, and the layers of concern and stress in the EPA employees' eyes said, "Believe me, I have thoughts and concerns."

I get to the traffic light near the gas station where my husband buys his chewing tobacco (he's from western Pennsylvania) which is his only vice and I realize I have forgotten my thermos of coffee. Also I'm freezing . . . this choice of jacket was terrible. Why do I even still own that wool thing? Should I donate it somewhere? Its green lining means something to me. Snaps. I have a hard time giving away wool. (I still think about my first fancy wool skirt, a deep Prussian blue with a lining, from high school bought at Marshall Fields in Chicago, when shopping downtown was a big special deal.) How I always feel like I will need wool when I am lost in the tundra, how when I am turned out of my village I will mourn every scrap of wool I gave away.

DO I GO BACK? Yes. I loop around the block, park, go in, get my thermos (pink, paint worn off a little worn around the rim), change jackets to my polar fleece—which weirdly matches my bag, all sort of purplish wine-colored, like "When I am an old woman I shall wear purple and look at me now!"—and then drive again. Wine-colored when I can't drink wine. The drug I'm on for rheumatoid arthritis, methotrexate, means I can't drink because it would be too hard on my liver, a once-a-week injection I often avoid and put off and make my dosage later and later even though I really don't have side effects because really, the shit used to be used for cancer treatment in higher doses, it's straight up poison, weakens the most precious system of defense and boundaries, the immune system, fundamental biological memory of past harms, but mine of course are over-reactive because my immune system is afraid. RA exploded right after the moment of maximum stress in my life, post-divorce after years of simmering at a slow burn. So now I accumulate the empty EpiPen-like hypodermics, which are partly clear and bulky, in plastic jugs and detergent bottles behind the dining room cabinet, then I'm supposed to duct tape the lids and throw the containers away with the trash where I worry they will end up in the ocean anyway.

AT THE STRATFORD TRAIN STATION, not even 6 a.m., I pull into the non-reserved spaces to the left of the platform, parking spot 110, and go to the machine to get a ticket. I keep entering 118, then eventually I do it right. I bought a train ticket on my phone yesterday on the app, which had stored a previous unused one-way trip from the action itself. I love the MTA phone app. I know I have to go to the Canal Street station from Grand Central. I'm going to be very early but that's okay. I am always trying to be as early as possible to the airport. I'm one of those people. I think once when I was little in the 1970s we had an all-family dash through the airport to get to a flight to Germany to see my mom's family, and the urgency felt, to my young unformed mind, like life or death, and my dad always got stressed out. I don't like the airport stress of having to show documents, how expensive the tickets are. Once I'm at an airport early and I'm at the gate, I feel free, unreachable. That's the vacation: nothing to do but sit. Sometimes when I'm stressed about something else

I'll have nightmares about being small and running through an airport, that the walk becomes impossibly long, that I can't move my little legs fast enough, that everyone is upset at everyone, that heaving feeling in your chest when you can't run anymore. But I also remember such nice times of travel when I was young: waiting in O'Hare for German relatives. There was a glassed-in walkway and you could look down into customs for your family coming through the lines and sliding their suitcases onto the tables for customs. In the plane they used to give every little kid a tiny plastic bag with toys inside, shaped like the bags that flight attendants used to carry, a half circle like a setting sun.

ON THE TRAIN PLATFORM, the sky is still the dark blue of 5:45 a.m. in November, waiting for sunlight. I open Twitter and someone named @Cruzkayne has written, "this isn't really what twitter is for, but ten years ago today my son died and I basically never talk about it with anyone other than my wife. it's taken me ten years to realize that I want to talk about it all the time. this is about grief." Then he's written a whole thread about grief. I retweet it because this is what Twitter is for, I think: beautiful stories of heartfelt experiences, sent out in tiny bits to the world, sent on and on to strangers. Grief and yet the joy of not being alone with the grief. I love Twitter because I mute and unfollow shitty people. And in the pandemic that we don't yet see coming, Twitter will turn into a lovesong, a dirge, of loss.

STANDING ON THE PLATFORM in the cold, the rushing sounds of I-95 in the background. There's that electrified track sound,

kind of a very high, very soft whistling like when a train is coming, the vibration of the metal. But no train comes and the
sound keeps going. It's not a train, it's my freaking tinnitus,
damage to my hearing either from too much loud music or from
TMJ, gritting my teeth from the stress of being me plus the first
stressful marriage, the dentist I went to in Columbus who told
me all my teeth were cracked but I didn't have dental insurance
so I left, half thinking they were trying to scam me, and what
were they going to do—replace all my teeth? They didn't tell me
that wearing a mouthguard might prevent splitting headaches,
so I waited literally ten more years before finally getting a dentist
who told me what was going on and that I needed jaw surgery,
which I never got. Anyway now I've always got this whistling
sound in the background. Sometimes if people talk softly I can't
hear them above the whistling, but it's not fixable so what can
I do, it's not pain, and I can live with it. The sound of a train
coming always makes me happy, so there's that, it's just confusing when I'm on a train platform.

I'm so tired, can barely even take in the NYT headlines on
my phone. "In Shift, US Says Israeli Settlements in West Bank
Do Not Violate International Law." Well, fuck you, you fucking
evil evil monsters. Do we even have international law? "Impeachment Investigators Exploring Whether Trump Lied to Muel-
ler." The impeachment hearings are going on right now but I
can't even watch them. I don't watch any of the Dem candidates'
debates, I didn't watch the political conventions in 2015, I just
can't. I start to yell and cry almost immediately. There's a way
in which I have to shield myself to function. I do read some of
the impeachment stuff and a lot of other news but I don't read
this article, but of course he fucking perjured himself, that's been

every single moment of this presidency, so the real question is whether there will be any kind of accountability at all.

"The Iran Cables: Secret Documents Show How Tehran Wields Power in Iraq." Images flash in my head of the 1990s, first Gulf War, streets of Minneapolis in the winter, shuffling in slush at protests, a dumpster on fire near some building, someone tipped over a newspaper dispenser, these snapshots that remain, Virginia Woolf's "moments of being," the way it makes me write because how else do you make sense of this string of beads as memory? It has to do with the way memory is stored, by theme rather than narrative, and so how hard it is to restring the beads into time sequences, the work of writing.

"Amazon Deforestation in Brazil Rose Sharply on Bolsonaro's Watch," I do click on this because it's the epicenter of impending human extinction, picture of a smoking landscape of ash dotted with glowing red embers, hellscape. "The Amazon rainforest in Brazil lost an area about 12 times the size of New York City from August 2018 through July of this year. . . a 30 percent increase from the previous year and the highest net loss since 2008." Fuck Bolsonaro too, Lula the leftist Brazilian former leader was imprisoned on trumped-up charges but now he's free but not in power, and the article points out that the rate of destruction overall has slowed since the 1990s, beef production. I let the image of the smoking Amazon hit me in the gut, the early morning dark, the sadness of what is actually happening on this smoking planet right now.

The train pulls up, its red lights spelling out Grand Central, and I feel a stutter of hesitation over which door to choose. Commuters and New Yorkers always seem to know. I go to the right with a crowd, walking forward in the aisle quickly, since I have to face forward so I don't get sick. I turn left into a row and slide all the way in. I love a window seat, love feeling cozy looking out at the gray gloom. I glance at an opinion piece from Cory Booker about how the Democrats shouldn't be so dogmatic about charter schools, and okay, that includes me. I save to read later. I'm pretty dogmatic about anything that labor unions have told me to think, and as part of the labor movement for so long, that's just my go-to, what I think first.

IN THE GOLD LIGHT inside the train I open the white laminated folder and take out one of my fountain pens from the zipper case I got at Target that looks like a slice of an orange. These things make me happy, and especially since the election there have been things to get me through the day, and I am more intent about any little thing that contains a light of happiness: fountain pens, happy colorful socks, lotions that smell nice. I love my little portable fountain pens. Uggggh there's the outline for the webinar, what am I even . . . why aren't I working on it, I did write down ideas last week, but I have to focus, it's tomorrow. I already wrote a book on this, I'm a teacher. I want to do well. Why does me doing well have to include a process of me going through a tunnel of doom? It's like part of me realized early on that I could make myself work and do well if I first scared the shit out of myself. Worst-case scenario, but the worst case is always that people won't approve of me. So clearly, in my heart of hearts I'd make a terrible iconoclast; I have to be rebellious with a crew who will grant me the approval I need as fuel. The live webinar writing workshop has more than 180 people registered, there's going to be a recording online, but probably only a third will tune in. The registration system of the US Pain Foundation was targeted by 5,000 bots who registered and took up all the spaces, so the organizer had to go back in and delete a bunch of them by hand. The bots will be watching, I guess, a fog of semi-people like how on Twitter the bots evolved into demonic hate-spewing.

When I give my talk, I have to ramp up into my public persona. I'm such a dork. How much bullshit it is, me pretending I know anything. (Welcome to the tunnel of doom. We'll be done soon.) It makes me want to cry, the fact that I pretend I know, that there's any kind of hope or order in the universe, that anything can lead to anything else, pretending there's hope in writing. I should tweet with another link to the webinar registration, do my schtick, which has morphed into being super-nice and using a lot of exclamation points and heart emojis, maybe to hide the fact that I'm a cynical depressed asshole. If I weren't me but I followed me on Twitter or knew me, I'd probably hate me, me and my enthusiasm, who gave you the right to talk about anything—like you know anything at all. This is what my hometown of New Lenox, Illinois, thinks of me, hahahaha they never think of me. Hometown taunts: *You think you're better than us because you went to a fancy private college out of state.* So why do I have these vestigial voices, why do I bully myself? Why save that hate and why do I keep such a candle for the Midwest? I preserve this voice inside me because I think if I'm ready, it can never surprise me. Jesus Fucking Christ, JFC thank you Zoloft. Honestly what would I have done without Zoloft since age 20? All the crying. JFC JFK KFC: an evil incantation to summon America. I tweeted that because it cracked me up, and it was not as appreciated by Twitter as I thought it deserved, but that's Twitter.

Am I even a good teacher? I don't know. Many people even doubt that creative writing as a discipline matters. I got promoted, but the truth is that some days I am so burned out I can barely function. I lived with eight years of a colleague's unpredictable anger, ego mania, and habits (older entitled white guy) and the intense harassment of the last year (same guy who conducted a public shaming of me because I dared disagree with him, even though I immediately backed down, but he still felt entitled to punish me for even opposing him privately for a moment). I'm doing everything that's asked, but sometimes my inbox is just a swarm of tasks in various compliance and outcomes databases that all make me want to cry. I've gained a little weight because I have been bribing myself with chocolate and my to-do lists to handle these tasks, to do the next right thing. So getting arrested at a protest was different, a real act chosen by me, not something I felt I had to do for someone else to keep getting a paycheck or to avoid being yelled at or getting a snippy passive-aggressive email.

Here, on this train, with everyone quiet, an engine pulling us down a steel track toward a glorious dirty city on the way to court, this is real. My students' essays, where I can see progress and something that, at least for this one class, undeniably matters. The intimacy of grading, the fact that I have to open up my own heart, the live unknowing of nonfiction, which is our research, I tell them: the work of looking into our minds and being honest about what is there, the emotional work of feeling it, the resistance to it, then the swimming in another person's experience and wondering what other people's lives are like. I look out the window at the clouds, which form a blue-gray mass over the Long Island Sound at Norwalk, and a slice of pale-yellow sunlight from the rising sun cuts underneath the gray along the water.

I didn't even know until a few weeks ago that I had to book Ivan's permit test online via an appointment calendar, and there were only a few slots available at a time. I could have made it for later but I wavered and then the later appointment was gone. There are so many things with mothering that nobody tells you how to do, that you just learn about as asides on Facebook.

Cliff is done teaching at the high school at a little after 2, though he also has to walk our dog Hazel. He doesn't get tense like I do about being late for things or ruining things. Parenting is very confusing and to be honest I cannot even imagine doing it before Google. When Ivan was young I was not on social media because Facebook had just started; I was on MySpace, but I didn't write anything about what was really going on in my life, living with rage and instability in my house and not able to pay our bills, and in Ivan's first three years I guess I made a lot of phone calls. I wrote in my journal.

I think with all the hell of the world now, I am fixated on Ivan having some normal-kid years, some chance to play and do his rites of passage. I am wishing his generation did not have to face this uncertain terrifying future, like a sucker punch they received even before conception.

I've been urging my son to look at an app that asks sample questions for his driving test, and his friend gave him the print-out of the Connecticut driving manual, a thick binder-clipped stack of copied pages. I don't know if I've ever seen my son study. Maybe once. We worried about his eyes, the effect of multiple concussions—a few from sports, a few from falling under his desk at indoor recess, getting tripped, and so on, he's athletic but very floppy and gangly—on the ability of his eyes to converge on print, the muscle control. An MFA student where I teach told me there was such a thing as vision therapy, and it seems like a very Fairfield County thing to do, and yet how sensible. It's something that so many kids probably need as much as gym class, the fine muscles of the eye that need help in working together and converging on focal points like a line of text. A blow to the back of the head waggles them out of alignment and makes them forget how to work in tandem, but then these simple exercises— so low-tech, focusing on a letter chart and moving it away from your face, converging your eyes until you see double—and then there's improvement and he could read better, his resistance to all the eye exercises, but how he really loved that one young female doctor, like they got each other, but then she left and he was kind of crushed but she left him a note to tell him to do well in school. How certain people get teenage boys and can really connect with them.

And how can he now be almost driving, that tiny curl of human I held against my chest on High Street in Columbus, Ohio, waiting for a bus and feeling like I'd never been so vulnerable in my life. *Wait, I have to defend two people now?* And now he's a real person, with nostalgia and memories and opinions and reflection. I don't know how to prove this but I think that nostalgia is one of the most important human emotions, as long as it's the kind that sees the flaws of the past, and even if it's nostalgia for the present moment that you might not get to enjoy as a memory in the future because you won't be around or we won't have a world. Foreshortened mourning the loss of entitlement to future nostalgia.

When I was the age my son is now, I was basically a version of who I am now, a bit too open-minded. In sophomore year of high school I had kind of an awful honors history teacher who made us read Allan Bloom's *The Closing of the American Mind* and as a result I decided I would do my part for the culture and just listen to classical music. Thank god that didn't last, but I was easily cowed and then easily resentful and rebellious when I figured out how wrong it was to not present two or seven sides to an issue, to present the grand narrative. He never gave us the counterarguments, was always yelling at us.

When I took my driving test, it was winter in Joliet, Illinois, and I wore a boxy blazer coat, white and gray, with shoulder pads in 1980s fashion, and I had my hair pulled back in a barrette. I kept the snipped-out photo from my first driver's license. I am looking with a hint of sarcasm or hoodedness at the camera, thin-faced and dark, all of 118 pounds. I was doing Jane Fonda videos after school because I was convinced I was fat, alarmed that the scale kept going up, when the truth was that I was tiny, same 5'3" height I am now.

Every era in a child's life—maybe especially or only with the first child—is like looking at a vast unplowed field. Am I doing this right, mothering? Every one of his birthdays I feel an odd sense of accomplishment, as in, he's still alive. His sharp face made up of his father's chin and eyebrows, my large sleepy brown eyes.

I open the folder with student essays, always nervous to dive into their heads. I want them to do well, maybe unreasonably so. The start of an essay is like a runner on the blocks. Try the hardest that you can. All I want them to do is to try on the page, and I can see the tracks of trying. That's one thing I can do at this point.

K. writes about her family moving away from the warmth of St. Thomas to the cold of Pittsburgh for her father's cancer treatment when she was six, but she didn't know at the time why they had moved to this cold snowy place, how she looked at the moon to retain a sense of connection to the natural world.

I have pushed her, and here in her minute beautiful detail the results are flowering. She's an artist, has written about her passion for painting and drawing, and we as a class have succeeded in pushing her to see how each scene in an essay can be concrete and visual, can use her astounding gifts in the visual sense. I will, after this, push her again to another draft in which she will recount the conversation with her mother about what it was like to relocate so far away so that her father could be pumped full of poison while her mother worked at the Dollar Store. Some of us will cry in class, seeing the results. It amazes me when students take on the missions and meet the dares I give them. This is the strength of good girls: they leap headlong, so willing to get guidance, so grateful when someone points in the right direction. The danger of good girls is that they will equally leap when pointed in the wrong direction. Maybe we feel like we don't have a choice.

A., a wiry student in her 60s with spiky hair dyed blue, writes about compassion in the chaos of her job, social work with teens, and she hunts herself, turns over the pages of her mind: expose, expose. She has honed in on the essay as meditation in the unpretty and vital way I love, pursuing the contradictions. She has gotten Phillip Lopate's command to capture the "mind at work" on full blast, and she manages to swing around to insights at the end of three pages of relentless churning in the key of life. The release we are all aiming for.

I keep checking the time. More commuters get on at a stop, and they are sleepy, in their pre-work zone. The oval white ridged light in the ceiling near the train entrance looks like a luminescent soap dish. People are sleeping or closing their eyes and resting as they stand, swaying slightly with the train movement. Most of them have hats on and are sheathed in layers of thick black and gray because it's cold. There's so much adrenaline and caffeine in me already, but beneath those chemicals I am tired. It's scary how often I think about retirement and I'm only forty-eight. It's a beautiful thing to be able to watch people turned in all directions either with their eyes closed or half-closed. You rarely get to just look at the unguarded faces of strangers. Everyone's energy is down low, conserving. It's so good that bodies can do this, go into sleep mode.

I write on the rubric for A.'s essay, a kind of graph that is a visual way for students to hopefully understand what they might focus on with a revision. Grading is both daunting and ridiculous. I am an easy grader, but really it's easy to either do great or terrible in my class, depending on whether you stay with the fierce current of trying. Still: what does it mean, this tiny difference between a 94 and a 96? I suppose it means something to me, a tiny nudge, my fear of shutting anyone down from their own creative development if they're trying something interesting. I get disappointed when an essay is just words on a page. I can tell if they've tried. And if they keep trying, they will improve. That's the one source of hope I have, which I then assume applies to other things besides essays, where it works most reliably. It doesn't always work in the non-essay world.

C. writes about her fear of swimming, and I see two things, no—three. I see her skill at almost field-note type observation.

I nudge her toward more reflection in her note, but that's an abstraction, and I haven't explained it right, because at the end of the semester in her letter, she will say that she doesn't know how to reflect, or worse, that she's bad at reflection, and I will know then that I didn't ask the right questions to show her that she *does* know how. The thousand little failures of teaching. How to prompt reflection—the asking of the question. I am tentative with her because I know she's tentative with herself and so brutal in her self-talk, has told herself she's not creative, and yet in workshop she asks the most devastatingly astute questions of other students. So . . . I can't get her there this semester, but I don't know that yet, sitting there on the train.

I look down at my bag and make sure it's upright against my leg and that nothing has spilled out including my overly high-protein snacks. I bought the bars and the drink yesterday at the health food store on the corner after I had my blood drawn at Quest. For the blood draw to check that my liver is okay on the RA drugs, I went into the spring-green waiting room, nicely redecorated, and sign in via iPad. I always try to type in my information as fast as humanly possible for no reason, as if I'm in a race and for once I know all the answers to the world's easiest quiz: my name! my birthdate! my phone number! The End! I win every time.

I have good veins, the reliable blue-purple line phlebotomists like, and if they are not too busy, they read my tattoo, which is on my left forearm and says "And it is good when you get to no further," which is from a John Ashbery poem I saw on a bridge in Minneapolis, and I know it's kind of pretentious, but it's also a good judge of character. People of all social classes who have been through hell look down to read it and then look up and me and say, "RIIIIGGGGHT?" Other people scan it and purse their lips and are mystified. To me it means a lot of things, but mostly it is a reminder that things end, that they must end, and that can be good.

I know the routine, to hand over my insurance card, take off my jacket, roll up my sleeve, hold it straight on the padded chair arm, and then I look away. It's just what I do. I've never fainted or anything, but it seems to hurt more if I watch the blood gushing into the tube. The phlebotomist put her finger on the gauze square and then told me to press the square for her while she got a piece of tape.

Yesterday I just felt ragged and edgy, a Monday, and I was so nervous for court, nervous I'd canceled class, nervous because it was the end of the semester and I was behind on all the tasks, nervous about getting back for Ivan's driving permit test and passing the test I make myself take every day of whether I'm a good mother.

BUT SO WHAT REALLY is the anxiety about today? Court seems kind of menacing and I have hardly even done anything criminal, but in my mind it had become big, and I think on some level my body believed it was going back to jail. It was not that I was scared of jail, exactly, but that I felt that I had to summon a degree of extreme focus to make sure I was down at the courthouse at the right time and place, and I was scared. Like I had to haul one second into the next and couldn't make a mistake. So after my blood draw I walked down to the health food store and bought two of the same kind of protein bars I bought when I was arrested, because having them in my bag felt like protection, as well as that terrible protein shake that I would end up not drinking for a few weeks.

As I sit now on the train going to court, my bag rests on my leg, and inside is a journal, so I pull it out and take a few notes, taking a break from grading. As I get out my journal I touch my case full of fountain pens, and my water bottle, and a zippered pocket that holds the form we are supposed to bring with us to court. I kept checking that pocket. Any required papers and forms make me very nervous. I suppose they make everyone nervous. Papers are just asking to be lost. Here, take this very very thin rectangle that the wind can easily blow away or that you can easily leave someplace or that can be mistaken for any one of a million other similar white rectangles.

There's supposed to be a lawyer there, in the building with us in court. I've only been to court a few times in my life. Once for a right turn on red when I wasn't supposed to turn. A cop in Statesboro, Georgia, pulled me over, and the truth is the reason I was distracted was that I was fighting with my then-husband about something. We lived there, in that hot town about an hour into the cotton from Savannah, and I taught at a university, in a place where the Civil War was still treated as a current event but the current wars in Iraq and Afghanistan weren't seen as controversial or noteworthy. The main military action on people's minds was Sherman mowing through Georgia to the coast. The stifling wave of heat on that land, navigating against the constant presence of other people's version of Jesus Christ, the "personal relationship with Jesus Christ" that came up so often, like people in the North talking about the weather, how I learned that even the progressive kids talked that way and I got used to it, except for the few pained kids, most of them queer, who'd been completely cut off from their evangelical families. I was grateful for the job because it gave me some stability, tenure-track, which I needed in order to figure out how to leave my then-husband. In the car we were having the kind of fight that more and more actually made me feel insane. The kind of fight where, even though no blows were exchanged, I felt physically exhausted and head-swimmy afterward.

I hated fighting with him in the car. Thank god I was driving because he was a road rager, but even being with him in the close bubble of the car was unnerving when he was angry, his sharp eyes. I think I'd been crying the night before—it was that day-after-sobbing feeling like I was just emptied of every ounce of connective tissue. So then I was distracted and turned right on a red light, my bad. But then the cop strode up and I rolled down the window, and I asked him whether there was even a sign about "no turn on red," and asking that question meant I was not a good southern girl (and there are badass bad southern girls too, of course) afraid of and yet adoring the police, and I did it in my non-southern accent and I said I worked at the university and those were all the wrong things to say. He gave me a ticket for a moving violation and I went to court, taking my grading with me as always, and someone had told me the cop probably wouldn't show up, but there he was, standing up there with his black boots laced up to his knees, his legs spread wide like he was a capital letter A with his arms crossed, and his red beefy face, and I said what I thought had happened, and he scoffed at me, sending waves of hate in my direction (what, was he mad about General Sherman still, or was I so tough I might take away his guns and abort a fetus right in front of him and kiss a girl?) and I had to pay a fine.

The other court appearance was the divorce a few years later. That was massive, a series of visits and actions over months, hiring a lawyer named April and borrowing money from my parents for some of the retainer, collecting binders of documentation and transcribing the text messages and abusive voicemails, the saga, prolonged arguments about custody and what kind of living environment our young son needed for visitation. There was a lot of panic, and the judge that day looked at my almost-former husband, and said to him sternly that he could no longer treat the mother of his child that way. My friend Sharad told me, "Document everything" and I didn't.

I'M WRITING NOTES ON THE TRAIN about today in a slim paperback notebook with a tan cover I bought in a pack of six from Costco when we were still members. They treat their workers better than BJ's, but we had waited to join Costco until when Bingo the now-dead cat got diabetes so we bought his insulin there because it was cheaper. Poor skeletal Bingo who in Georgia would slink out of the cat door and would drag squirrels and other creatures into our house and we'd hear him crunching their bones. We'd wake up and find the bodies of creatures, decapitated clean at the neck because he liked the heads best, little truffles of brain, I guess. It was so sad after he got sick in Connecticut, the routine of injecting him in the back of the neck, I let him suffer too long because I'd never had to put an animal to sleep, and it came down to having an argument with a vet who wanted him to stay alive, so we switched vets to someone who took one look at Bingo and said, "Oh, it's time." He was such a good good boy, stripey noble black-gray tiger, a stray from Columbus with shoulders and swag and a stroll like a mountain lion. I named him and have always been proud of that because Bingo is a perfect name for a cat.

Could I ever even write about today or the action? I didn't even tweet that I was arrested, because I feared that even though I've got tenure, it could turn into a big thing at the Catholic university where I teach if a right-wing troll were to get ahold of it, the death threats that my friend Kris got for teaching about whiteness, the task force on freedom of expression afterward that tried to push against the idea that "freedom of expression" gets twisted into "equal air time for both sides" and into "let's let the most fringe right-wing speakers talk." But maybe I'll write about it because nobody will bother to read a whole essay, so this content will be safe. I had to sign a form when I took a job in Georgia attesting that I'd never been part of an organization to advocate for the overthrow of the government. If anybody wanted to make that case, they could have read my first book to tell stories about my anarchist youth, which was mostly very tame zine-making and writing and long meetings with a collective and occasional protests. I checked "no" on that form and kind of felt like I was lying but also not.

At Stamford the ray of pale yellow is gone and the gray is slightly illuminated and meets the water at the horizon like a shade pulled shut against the blue-gray water. My general ever-present feelings of guilt sharpen to a point: it was small, but I'd committed a crime. My fear of being yelled at, awareness of how easy it is to fold when someone is angry at you. Then again, being put in a situation where this crime was the only logical or ethical option.

A train horn sounds from up ahead. I go back to grading essays, which requires a kind of extended opening of my soul's eyeball or ear. I have to hold open that watching/listening organ and wait for the slightest resonance, Woolf's "oyster of perceptiveness, an enormous eye" that she describes in her essay "Street Haunting." This is what grading essays is about: watching for the sentences to ring something in my soul. This is also the purpose of the essay, to open the shell from around the soul, to clear back the illusion of single view, a simple persona, an easy answer, a too-strong thesis. To disrupt the tracks of the mission-driven, to-do-list ego and its harshness, its clinging to opinion. The essay in its questioning and wandering has helped open space for spirituality and not-knowing in my life, or maybe it's the other way around, that I am also drawn to the opposite of the to-do list, the meditative state, and so that's what I love most about the possibilities of the essay. I guess the essay, like all art, lets us project all of our manifestos onto it. My main discovery is the relief of not-knowing, not having to know, in pockets of text first and then tentatively in pockets of life, though living it is so much harder.

J.'s essay on friendship and illness is advanced, stunning: she's built a world here, a sophisticated attempt to see what she herself was thinking, examining text messages during a time when she sought a diagnosis for a complex health problem while she was only a teenager. What I have to do when I read a student's essay is hold open the cage of my heart. That makes me think of John Cage, his song "4'33"" that is just silence, the overlaps in his life between Dadaism and Buddhism. There's a book about his life, *Where the Heart Beats,* that I bought hardcover because I just needed it so much. The open cage of the heart, how dad's sternum looked as a raised stitched ridge after they'd gone in to do the emergency triple bypass two months ago. I bought a ticket to fly out to Illinois because at first he wasn't going to do the surgery and then we would have had to wait for the next heart attack, how much that visit took out of me, the hospital time, but also how good it was to be there, trying to help, at the new Silver Cross Hospital a mile and a half north of my parents' house. I'd been a candy striper volunteer in an actual white-and-red-striped smock at the old Silver Cross in Joliet in high school, because of course I was, good girl, and the old hospital was dank and old and oddly designed or added onto with dead-end hallways that were confusing to navigate and the carpet had been disinfected so many times it smelled slightly rotten. Everyone in our town always said, "If you go into Silver Cross, you might not come out." But then much later when I was twenty-eight I was home for a visit and ended up getting admitted with a kidney infection, 105 fever, almost died, and they did save my life. So anyway, the hospital where we fix our bodies, the pages where we see ourselves in X-ray. Despite the love I have of these essays, I am also always counting pages, seeing how many more I have to read, how many essays, because it's a strain, keeping this awareness open, and I also want to be at the end.

Sometimes the cage of the heart flies open of its own accord like a butterfly's wings. Am I sharpening my students' tools for surgery or butterfly catching? Nabokov hunted butterflies, wandering the forests around his family's Russian estate, then went into exile, which he writes about in the book *Speak, Memory*, which I read with my undergraduates in Georgia and boy, did they complain, but they also loved it. Language can do that, the power and peril of stringing words together, the way they can open the heart or infuse it with hate and lock it in so many cages, presidential tweets and fake ads. I'm done with grading, the relief of the rib cage snapping shut. I sip my coffee, shrug my shoulders, feel the privacy of my protective persona, my functional self, closing around me.

I CHECK MY EMAIL, reply to an advisee. 7:42 a.m.:

> Dear M.,
> Great to talk to you yesterday! I believe that if you didn't get a degree, you can just input "no degree awarded." I've cc'd Sharon in graduate admissions who can help you with any questions you have about transcripts and the application itself.
> Thanks!
> Sonya

I always write with too many exclamation points in my emails, which is a documented thing that women do, so some people think it's the worst thing ever, women emoting too much all over the place, but I don't give a shit, bureaucratic communication is abrasive especially for students, so I want to be a human, and exclamation points are free, I'll use as many of them as I want. I kind of caught it from my effusive mother-in-law in Pennsylvania whom I adore, who took on Ivan and me from the moment she met us, as did her husband, and Ivan is their grandkid as if by biology, thank god. She wrote emails with lots of exclamation points and then I started doing it back to her, because mirroring is what we do to get in sync as rhythmic social beings, subconsciously, so why not also in writing, and then I began to do it more. If a man judges me for being an airhead because of it, then all the better for me, because I don't forget it when I'm underestimated.

A MAN SITS DOWN on the seat farthest from me on the train bench, then another man sits in the middle next to me, wearing a red ski beanie, in a dress shirt and wool coat, ready for work, and we smile at each other, and then he puts on a sleep mask and leans his head back. He has a slight scruff of whiskers that I think is fashionably intentional. The train goes into the city, sliding among the close canyon of brick buildings and then underground, the darkness with occasional lights as the train pulls to a stop.

We end beneath Grand Central Station. I look at the man next to me, who is still out cold with his sleep mask on and his head leaned back. I glance at the guy on the aisle seat as if to ask, what do I do? He kind of half-glances at me but is busy getting up and putting on his coat. People are gathering their things. I poke the man gently but firmly twice in the shoulder of his wooly overcoat. He looks around, foggy, eyes swimming as he emerges from a deep sleep. He was just in dreamland and is about to get up and stagger through the crowd in Grand Central.

And then people flow out of the doors onto the narrow cement platform, the underground gray-black ceiling, amid heat from the train engines, and every time I step onto the platform here I always get a surge of energy and disbelief, like *Look at me, I am navigating!* The ability to get off a train and be somewhere else entirely makes me feel proud of myself, as if I have gotten to the place through my own power. And the crush of people's forward-motion, the focused wanting and propelling, the gathered bags each holding folded tasks and food for the future and umbrellas and tissues and gum and subway cards and pens and necessary tools for potential situations. I remember living in Boston and having to take stuff with me for the whole day, work and after work and errands, in many tote bags, and planning my day in a series of loops, always with a book. The crowd is compressed through the open train doors and onto the narrow platform like water sprayed through a nozzle, and we pass a sign of Caution on the wall, and then dispersed outward into the high held space of Grand Central which really is grand, from a time—why is it so far away now?—when we knew how to build curved spaces that seemed to mirror our skulls or burrows or fruit, things that used to protect and feed us. How would you describe the color of the ceiling? When I first saw the constellations painted there I was amazed, and still am. What a beautiful gift. It's a blue like the box from the jewelry store Tiffany's but not exactly, a little more toward green or turquoise. Why don't we call it Grand Central blue? Because that would be incredibly New-York centric, but then again, so is Tiffany's.

And sure, the painting of stars and constellations was likely not "cost effective" and was extra and was therefore a kind of compounded extended care that paid forward and touched and twinkled. There's the curve of blue, some constellations of shapes or mythological gods whose identities I never take in, never study, instead it's just the fog of blue, and the staircases with marble banisters that go up and down on either side of the hall, and the changing list of destinations, red and green names, times, and windows and the round kiosk in the middle girded with slots holding train schedules and a person inside who can unsnarl the tangled traveler. The spray of human traffic is shunted into other streams, dodging shoulders and peripheral vision and touch sense of vibrations and buffeted noise that prevents collisions, the dodging of the ghost of contact, swirl of coat and shape of dark bag, step left, step right.

I am so happy I don't have to rush. I have plenty of time to get to the subway and then take the 6 train down to Canal Street, but I'm still anxious because of the steps I have to take, even though I know the way. Part of it is that because of joint pain, which saps my energy so I'm like an iPhone with a wonky battery, which means I have to be efficient. I walk down a marble hallway lined with fancy chocolate stores and stationery shops toward the subway, proud that I have been coming down to New York enough that I know my way, past the snack and newspaper place and down the steps.

I refill my MetroCard for the way back. I think about everyday extravagance, how I'm able to do things like put $10 on a MetroCard because there might be a future, how I'm able to buy things I want, remembering buying shampoo and conditioner at the Dollar Store, everything at the Dollar Store, Suave shampoo, going to stores with Ivan to buy dented cans of vegetables and beans on clearance. By age two and a half, he would reach for a toy on the shelf, look at me, and say to himself with his pink little lips and thoughtful soft face, "Too 'spensive." How I see new stuff for toddlers and kids in stores, fresh in boxes and with bright colors, and I want to buy everything for that kid even though he's a teenager now because I couldn't buy anything new when he was younger, everything secondhand and garage sales, but I happen to be a Jedi-level garage-saler and thrifter, taught by the best, my mother, who could literally summon whatever you might desire from a garage sale.

I learned to go with her when I was young and found the delight and intimacy of stepping into someone's garage or driveway and smelling the smells of their house, seeing on tables a collection of objects that is like an essay: here are the things that I was drawn to or given and that no longer serve me, but yet that I think are worthwhile enough to put a sticky price tag on, even if it's a ritual nod toward a price of 25 cents. The fact that garage sales show you more variety and surprise than you could ever see anywhere but a thrift store, the adventures, how I found a cut-out black silhouette of an Indonesian boat in a frame in Georgia, how you could tell who had traveled, the solemnness of an estate sale, Jesus Fucking Christ how at one point in Columbus I bought a mattress from an estate sale, literally a mattress that someone had died owning, and I slept on that goddamn thing that had a divot in the middle where an aged body had curled in sleep. Being good at garage sales allowed me to look much more middle-class than I often was, and I have an unerring grasp of high-quality fabrics and materials, earrings and tunics, the way people of all the thousand invisible class distinctions in America can feel class in their bodies but we aren't allowed to name the seventy-four social classes that exist because it would take away the central illusion of "opportunity" that we need in order to function.

My old MetroCard is expired, so the machine replaces it with a new card that is pink and has a Shopbop ad on the card, whatever that is. I remember subway tokens from when I first came to New York City, made of a metal of one color at the edge with a design of some scrollwork, and then a different color metal with a hole in the shape of a Y in the middle, which was amazing because you could reach into your pocket or your bag and sort amid coins for the tokens without looking at them, pressing your flesh into the Y, making a paired puffy Y from the skin of your fingertip. I still always feel so proud to understand how to navigate even small bits of this city, remembering before the apps how people would tell me what trains to take and I'd be that person unfolding the huge map and tracing the colored noodles up and down Manhattan. Look at me, a woman who first came out to New York City as a Midwestern college student to stay with a friend for a few weeks during one summer vacation. I came down to New York after taking a class at a social ecology anarchist institute at Goddard in Vermont, where I'd carried around a UTI from having sex too many times with my college boyfriend and went to rural ERs over and over because there wasn't a health clinic nearby when all I needed was the right antibiotic. I got prescribed something I was allergic to and watched hives creep up my skin like footprints, feeling so sad and lonely at that place I thought would be a paradise. I was shy and didn't want to smoke weed and so the hippies were kind of mean to me, mostly that one white guy with a beard and long hair, I guess because I was too earnest to be cool. I don't know why I didn't want to smoke weed, but you know how it is, when that's the center of someone's identity, they feel really really threatened when you say "no thanks."

At the social ecology anarchist camp I read a lot of radical anthropology in the library that felt like a tree house and I bought an orange votive candle at the food co-op and a ton of cranberry juice to try to cure the UTI, sat at the expansive window in our large dorm room near my roommate's freshly built worm composter; she was in the sustainable agriculture class and seemed to feel sorry for me that I wasn't cool. The other girl J. was willowy and muscular and said we should do some contact improv dance, but I guessed that was kind of making a move on me, and although she was beautiful I didn't have that attraction to her that makes you want to reach out as if it's irresistible, didn't often allow myself to feel that with women, to relax into them, even though I'd already kissed a girl by that point. The most amazing moment at the institute was one day in an anthropology class that met in a kind of odd classroom shed. A swarm of bees decided to relocate and they covered the building, and the windows were blanketed with bees and we were inside, the whole building buzzing and vibrating with sunlight coming through the bees' bodies and wings, a honey-colored shadow. I don't remember how we got out, though I kind of remember deciding we would make a break for it and run.

So then after Vermont I came down to New York and stayed with my friend Blue from college and had a panic attack and burst into tears the first time I stepped into a silvery subway car as people piled in at rush hour. The jamming of limbs, the fact that I didn't know what was supposed to happen next. During the day when I didn't know what to do with myself while Blue was at work, I went to this amazing church near her parents' apartment called St. John the Divine, the church that was said to be under construction until there was no more poverty in the world. In the cobalt blue light coming in through the round stained glass windows, I sat in a pew and read an old paperback copy of Marge Piercy's *Woman on the Edge of Time* with the pages kind of rough and gold-colored like paperbacks from the 1970s.

ON THE SUBWAY, on an edge of time decades later, I count my stops. I know Astor Place with its sculpture of a large metal cube that rotates on one point out in the middle of an intersection. I remember one time I met O. there so long ago, watching the punks come up from a basement haircut place with colored mohawks, so now whenever I think of Astor Place I think of her, how she used to crack up at things I said that I didn't understand were funny.

I get off at Canal Street. I've been reading about the history of New York, so I learned the Dutch layer of history to this place, how Wall Street was established by Dutch traders as the fur trade and European disease began their creeping violence to Native communities. The bottom of Manhattan Island where it was first densely settled has streets with Dutch names like Amsterdam and Bleeker. I look at Google maps on my phone and the arrow kind of flips around amid the gray blocks and I'm not sure where I am. Walking toward the courthouse I pass a beautiful old building, maybe a firehouse, with big red doors and red sills and ornamental swirls or hooks of stone or metal on the roof. The sidewalk is made of slabs of old granite. Water has pooled from thousands of rains over the centuries, wearing shallow bowl-shaped depressions into the stone, the oldness, the smell of wet stone, the sizzle of tires on wet asphalt. I pass a Starbucks and walk under some scaffolding made of pipes and boards that drip water. I loop around and I can't get Google maps to give me walking directions. Lafayette Street—weird memory of an eighth grade presentation when I was Marquis de Lafayette; there was something about a powdered donut, I can't for the life of me remember why a filled donut was part of the presentation—maybe it was a joke on my powdered hair, curled to look like a wig? As Lafayette I talked about how impressed I was by America's potential, and how gathering together in social groups and clubs was part of the nascent country's democratic genius. In the fall of 2019 it looked to me as though we'd run that potential of the country into the ground.

I stop and put my coffee thermos on a brass double-headed fire spout, which I think is beautiful because it's been painted and repainted with chipped layers of different greens. I think about taking a picture, but then I also think somehow that stopping to take a picture of something beautiful right now is bad luck, like I'm saying that I'm appreciating things, as if this is some kind of a pleasure trip, when it's serious and I don't want to jinx it.

I go around a bunch of gray stone administrative buildings, checking and rechecking my phone until I find the courthouse, and there's an inscription about balance and fairness on the high part of granite walls that face outward on either side of the doorway. Despite the quote, the granite and the recessed entryway in cold stone leave me with the feeling of being tiny and scared. I want to take a picture of the quote because it says something about the rule of law that is, in these Trumpian days, almost nonsense, but then that's what many people have faced since before the beginning of this country, democracy for some. I am nervous and yet I am so supported, the full freight train of my white middle-class life and connections behind me, how easy this is for me, how many resources I have, and how many people come in here in terror, or not even able to read that inscription.

I go through the metal detector, surrender my bag, ask at a big square information desk where to go to get to area "D," and it's straight back along a hallway lined with old wooden benches and then to the left. I follow the hall and see Y., who I saw at the action, sitting on one of the wood benches like a church pew. She is so calm and centered as she smiles and waves, and it's nice to see her, but the introvert part of me wanted to sit somewhere and be alone, as long periods of chatting with strangers are tiring. Or that I tire myself out by feeling like I have to entertain and charm people to distract them from how weird I am. Yet I want to do more actions to be around her, and she makes me think about the edgy/doomy energy I always feel like I exude as an activist, the tension of getting it all perfect or knowing it won't work. Her very being—open, present, calm—is a kind of activism that draws people in without being a put-on "I'm so centered" hippie new-age sham. Something about the wide structure of her face feels European, German to me. She's wearing cat-eye glasses, and her short dyed-red hair swoops down over one eye.

I allow my body to relax against the wood of the bench in this lit stone anteroom outside of a courtroom. I am in the courthouse. For me—a person who is always transposing numbers, forgetting things, and worrying about being late—the hardest part is done.

Y. looks through her messenger bag, which is full of stuff and looks heavy, and she realizes she doesn't have the form they gave us when they let us out of jail, a sheet they said we had to bring back on our court dates. When she realizes she doesn't have it, after checking various folded and zip pockets in her bag, she doesn't get into a frenzy of throwing things out of the bag, and she doesn't say anything at all to berate herself.

She laughs and says, *I even put it on the table in a Ziploc bag. And then I forgot to grab it, the most important thing.*

I do that kind of stuff all the time, I say. She asks to see my form, which I had folded up carefully into sixteenths and tucked behind my credit card in the tiny zip-up wallet on the back of my phone case, which is more Grand-Central blue than Tiffany blue.

The concern in my house was that I'd miss the court date and forget the form. As soon as I came back from jail, I told Cliff I had to bring the form and had to go to court on a certain date, and he looked at me and we knew this was going to be a tiny opportunity for catastrophe. Somehow when I use my online Google calendar, I often transpose dates and phone numbers. Anytime I have to copy down a long string of numbers, everything is transposed without fail. I have made errors, producing issues and inconveniences, by putting dates into the calendar wrong and by reading the calendar wrong even after looking at it multiple times in pixels right in front of my eyes, and it seems like the more nervous I am about the appointment, the more likely I am to mess it up. My therapist had the same issue and had to go back to using a paper calendar. I don't want to carry any more notebooks around, but I get it. There's something about writing by hand, and the look of each written calendar page, that creates a visual, and I'm good with remembering and picturing information that is written, but not data, not at all. So Cliff and I reminded each other of the date, and I had him look at the form and double-check the calendar entry I'd made.

Y. looks at my form, and then says she's going to ask someone here at the courthouse about how to get hers printed out. That seems like such a reasonable response; I think I'd be crying and panicking a little. But then again, she's done this before. She asks if I will watch her stuff. She's wearing an actual real fur coat. Did she inherit it or get it as a gift? I sit for a while by myself next to her bag and the big coat, and I scroll through email and then think about the tense muscles in my shoulders and try to relax. I check the time.

She comes back with a printout of her form. I tell her a little about my writing and she tells me how she is an artist and how she's into participatory performance art, how she likes to bring art outward to interact with strangers. How much delight people can have when they know they're allowed to be silly and make things up inside an interaction that is categorized as "art." It reminds me of the delight my writing students have when they realize they have permission to think like this, to be funny and tangenty and emotional and serious and have ideas, all in a beautiful mix. They look at me every semester in shock to learn that this kind of writing is ever allowed, and I worry that we have edged this wild surprise at writing out of existence in a taxidermy of genres.

Y. and I both get excited as we talk about that space where possibility happens. It makes sense that she's into performance. During the Times Square action where we both got arrested, she showed up as a glorious pirate with a kind of pirate hat with a big plume and a patch, playing on the nautical theme. Did she also have a feather boa or am I just making that up?

I WASN'T NEAR HER during the action itself. She was one of the last to get put into our police wagon, so she must have been around the side of the boat or maybe on top of it. When we were trained for arrest, we had been told to put our hands behind us when we were handcuffed, and if we refused to do what the police said, we could face additional charges, so we were counseled not to resist. The police led us by the elbow and handcuffed us with the zip ties from behind, and because I have bad wrists due to rheumatoid arthritis, I decided to wear a carpal tunnel wrist brace with a metal splint, which was the best thing I did that day. I also had the presence of mind to hold my wrists facing outward rather than stretching them to face each other, a tip someone had shared at the meeting, because having your wrists facing is harder on your shoulders and allows less room for your hands to move.

I didn't like the look of the white guy who was our arresting officer, you could tell he was annoyed and disgusted by us, a youngish guy with dark hair and a kind of round face with small squinted eyes who would not make direct eye contact. They separated women from men. He and a few other officers led us in a long line near a full-length white school bus that they were filling slowly with men who were arrested, and we watched as they photographed the men one by one and as other police crews worked to detach people from the boat. Because of the layers I was wearing, I was standing there sweating in the sun. My hands were behind my back so I couldn't itch my face, pull my hair out of my face, or push my glasses up, and that level of discomfort forced me not to zone out. We stood in a line in our handcuffs and then after they handcuffed us, they asked for our IDs, which was ridiculous, because we couldn't get them so then we had to tell them which pocket to look in, so a female police officer went digging in our pockets, and my license was in a zip pocket of my polar fleece coat.

After the handcuffs were on, it was a different kind of experience, more tinged with pain and tightened muscles and having to pay attention. Suddenly we wanted things to go faster and they were going so slowly. They led some of the women over to a smaller windowless wagon, and one by one they checked us off and told us to get into the wagon, then where to sit on the benches along the sides, and then a woman came in and buckled us one by one into seatbelts. The women police officers were very gentle and courteous, and there was even something tender about the vulnerability of buckling a seatbelt over someone's belly while their hands are fixed behind their back, but it was not fond, because you're powerless, and it was clear: if they didn't like us, if we weren't a load of middle-class white women, they could do anything. One by one we were checked off and slotted into place on the metal benches, with R. next to me. A young wide-eyed woman with long blonde hair who was kind of loud and who had decided to do this action at the last minute told a story I don't remember, and a loud French foreign exchange student who had taken the bus up from North Carolina wondered how she could make the greatest impact for the revolution and if she should quit school.

Then Y. was loaded last into the wagon, and it seemed like a sign of kindness that one of the policewomen put Y.'s plumed black pirate hat back on her head after buckling her in. We were all realizing that the central issue, with our hands clasped tightly behind us, was how to sit to take the pressure off our shoulders. The door slammed, and then a second outer door slammed so that the back window was covered and dark. We were twelve or thirteen of us shoulder to shoulder in a tight metal space that was dark, with no back window, and that seemed to get warmer and warmer. We sat for what felt like at least an hour, but afterward, I figured out that it was only an hour total between the time we were handcuffed and the time I was booked into jail.

We sat in the close dark and each introduced and re-introduced ourselves. Everyone talked about where they were from and why they did the action. A woman who came down from her farm in Vermont was there with her husband on her grandson's second birthday. I gritted my teeth and closed my eyes when the loud French student started talking, as the noise seemed to echo in the small metal space and I felt nauseous. I tried to breathe and focus on my muscles, telling them to relax. And then Y. said to the French girl that it was important to keep our energy calm.

I said each person's name to myself under my breath try to remember it. The wagon smelled slightly of metal with an undertone of sweat, and the heat seemed to rise from our bodies. Someone mentioned Sandra Bland, the Black woman murdered by police in Texas. To think that she was all alone when she was killed, alone with policemen who cared nothing for her story or her life. And she'd done nothing, blameless and murdered, where we had stopped traffic at one of the busiest intersections in a major city, glued and chained ourselves to things, by choice. Sandra was just trying to get somewhere she wanted to go to start a new life.

Y. said into the silence that this was the hardest part, and it got warmer in the van, and R. itched her nose on my shoulder. I could feel trickles of sweat on my forehead, pieces of hair sticking to my face, the tendons in my shoulders aching. I tried sitting more upright to take the pressure off my wrists, kind of arching my back. Then I tried to lean back against the metal wall of the wagon, which helped but then hurt my lower back. I tried to lean forward. C., who has shoulder trouble, sighed and said she was in a lot of pain, and the woman next to hear said she could lean against her. I pushed up my glasses against R.'s shoulder. R. said she could lead us in a relaxation meditation, which ended up being amazing, reminders to imagine ourselves in a calming place, to focus on relaxing groups of muscles. We could see daylight through the front grate of the wagon, which had a window into the truck's cab through which we could see out the windshield, and people crossed in front of the parked vehicle. One of the women tried to assess whether the people were part of the action and what was happening outside.

Then the woman who was looking forward said, "Oh my god, the cops are watching porn on their phone." There were murmurs from everyone all at once. I had caught a glimpse of the dark shiny rectangle held by one of them up in the truck's cab, but I shrunk away from it and closed my eyes. It's just not what you want, to be a bunch of women handcuffed in the back of the truck while the cop driver is watching porn. Someone asked, *Are they doing it on purpose to fuck with us?*

The young girl with blonde hair and a wide-eyed impulsive look started yelling at the cops really loud, the noise seeming to fill the entire back of the wagon like a sonic fog, physically painful as it ricocheted off the metal and onto our eardrums. We had to yell at her to stop, tell her, *Do you know they could do anything or charge you with additional stuff to get you to be quiet?* We reminded each other that everything was being recorded and that we shouldn't talk about the organization or other actions. We sat for what felt like a long time as they dismantled the boat. Seconds ticked. Someone made a joke and a few others laughed nervously, and through the metal of the wagon we tried to filter traffic noise from the sounds of doors slamming, the scraping of chains that might have been the boat. Another person explained that the police had to block off all the streets between here and the jail so that all the police vans could leave together, but now I don't think that was true. It was fascinating how quickly rumors spread. We felt the wagon get shifted from park and accelerate, and we began moving.

Eventually the police van parked at the jail, and we sat there in the dark for another unknown period of time. We were then unbuckled one by one, with inscrutable long pauses when we were just sitting there, looking at each other. We were herded out of the wagon and then walked over to a large concrete yard with an overhang, ringed with chain link, like an old warehouse, and we stood in a line around the edges, waiting one by one to be processed.

I stood next to C., who was complaining about her shoulder hurting, and then she told a story about having her appendix burst inside her and not knowing it, going on with her day and cleaning her apartment because someone was coming over to interview her for NPR for some reason, and then she went in the hospital and her insides were a mess. So she was saying this pain in her shoulder from the weird angle of the handcuffs hurt worse than a burst appendix, and we asked the guard if he'd uncuff her, or cuff her in front, which we'd heard might be an option.

Our arresting officer stood there and said, "This is my first time doing this," which I believed, but which someone else told me later was a lie because she'd seen him before. He just didn't want to be a person with a real story to any of us. A woman on the other side of C. tried to dig her shoulder into C.'s shoulder as a way to disrupt the pain or loosen her muscles. And then I started asking C. about her family and her activist work, so she told me a long story about organizing and teaching, and I asked her about her husband, who it turned out taught writing like I did and who worked with a journal called *Radical Teacher* which I had read, so we talked about some of the heroes in writing instruction, like Peter Elbow, who is a long-time advocate of writing in a way that allows people to find their real voices and that doesn't disempower them. I kept asking C. questions to distract her as she winced, and I told her about my writing and my books, which I like to keep to myself unless it seems necessary because I don't want to seem braggy or derail the conversation, and her face lit up because we were in the same extended family of writer-teacher-activists.

As the line crept slowly forward toward the jail, more people kept arriving from wagons and on busses, sixty of us or so in all, with our hands behind our backs, subdued, exchanging occasional phrases quietly, breathing deeply, or doing whatever it was we needed to do to get through the tightness and discomfort of the awkward position. When C. got a little panicked, the cop came over, and I think he was worried she would start to make a scene, so he said that he couldn't uncuff her, but if she clasped her hands, that would relieve some pressure on her shoulders, and when she did that, it helped momentarily. Then we inched upward toward the front, and we were against the wall of the building, and we both leaned our upper shoulders against it and it felt better. Everyone was subdued and people's faces were sweating a bit. One of the people waiting across the edge of the courtyard was a guy in Buddhist monk's robes, and another was the guy Sean I had sat next to during the action. Eventually a group of us, the group of five from our arresting officer, were culled out of the front of the line, and the cops directed us where to go with touches to the back and shoulder and looks and turns of their bodies, and we were very careful, tired and jumpy, and we didn't want to do anything physically that they didn't tell you to do because they could do anything.

One at a time we walked through the doorway. Inside there was a printer—a printer! I got excited to see office supplies. And to the left was a podium where a very annoyed female police officer was taking down the same repetitive information over and over on forms to mark our entry into the facility. Then they printed a copy of the form. She asked me where I lived and I told her Connecticut, and then she asked me for my local address in New York, and I didn't have one, and she seemed confused, and I worried that was going to cause a problem, but then she kept going and I had to pose with the arresting officer for a second picture, like the worst prom ever, and then I was led to stand next to the printer, and then one by one we were led through a grim dirty gray lobby, windowless, seemingly dug from a cave, like a set from the show *Barney Miller,* that old cop show with the character Fish. My mom loved that show and so I did too, but now I've read stuff that says that these cop procedurals do something to our brains, making generations of people identify with police instead of with the things the police are doing wrong. Anyway everything in this jail looked like it was from the 1940s and never cleaned or only cleaned with dirty mop water, and a cop to my left in between two partitions was cutting open a windbreaker, slitting the hell out of it, to get out the drawstring, but there was no one nearby who might own the windbreaker. There were people in uniforms standing around and behind a long desk in the dim fluorescent light, and we were steered to the left to wait in a hallway near filing cabinets. It was scary in here—not in a "You scared me!" kind of way, but in a way where you could disappear in the dark amid these dense walls. The waiting was mysterious, long periods where nothing seems to happen. I leaned against a wall in the brown hallway stacked with filing cabinets.

A young lanky woman with long reddish hair waiting ahead of me in line told me a quick version of her current life, but I retained none of it, though I think it involved traveling around and doing activist stuff and couch-surfing. I remembered when that was possible, in my 20s, activists just crashing with each other, sleeping on the couch in various rented houses, and if you stayed too long another housemate would get mad, chore wheels, that time when a super-nice guy from the anarchist collective in Minneapolis stayed with me outside Boston, except I was living in a house of lesbians, I thought I was one but then I kept hooking up with guys, so after a few days the lesbians told me my friend Wayne had to leave, but he was there to give a talk I'd organized at a food co-op about the politics of environmental contamination and he had bad chemical sensitivities, had to wear a mask, and I remember taking him to Bread & Circus or the food co-op and he would smell an apple to see if it would aggravate his system. I hope he's okay wherever he is now. The lesbians asked him to leave, well, really, it was the lesbian in charge who cleaned the house daily, who I had many disagreements with and who must have been horrified at my slovenly ways and my adopting a cat who I had to leave alone during the nights because I worked the overnight shift at a group home. So the cat would cry all night, the cat I named Jersey because New Jersey is the Midwest of the East Coast. And the woman threatened to call the ASPCA, and I wrote a mean poem about her and stuck it to my door. Yes: a mean poem on the door of a rented third-floor room in a lesbian co-op house. Eventually Jersey went with me to another co-op of queer women, and then I moved in with the socialist guy in Dorchester. And then when I broke up with him, he got the cat.

Anyway, in the hallway, the red-haired girl, who somehow seemed like she could be a guitarist in a Led Zeppelin cover band, that vibe, told me that everyone from out of state was being sent to Rikers Island. Where would you hear that and why would you tell someone that? Clearly, though, I wasn't being sent to Rikers, as I was already processed here. I shoved down my fear because I thought they might have mentioned something like that in the training if it were true. They did mention that if you had meds, the cops could send you to a hospital to take them, so not to bring meds unless absolutely necessary. I didn't want to go to Rikers or the hospital. I thought about these activists living the full-time activist life, and how the normal Fox News world doesn't know about them at all, they think we are all paid by George Soros, but I even tried to get a grant from the Soros foundation and it didn't work, how we've been under the radar my whole life, the huge demonstrations against the first Gulf War and how I don't know if they ever made it onto the news, the idea being after the 1960s that if it didn't show up on the news, it didn't exist, and boy was that a sadly effective way to erase activism from the public consciousness.

One by one we inched forward along the dark corridor, as each person was called through a doorway into a darker hall where two female cops were collecting the contents of people's pockets. I let C. go ahead of me but then in my secret heart of hearts was sad about that in the extra minutes I waited, as I was sent backward to the end of our small line. Finally two women cops who seemed nice and normal and friendly asked me to turn around, and they snipped off the plastic cuffs and my arms floated upward. I was focused on being obedient and following their instructions, yet kind of groggy, and I got confused when they asked me to take various things off: the thin gray scarf wound around my neck, which they put into a manila envelope. I got to see my hands devoid of rings, everything left at home. I like rings because my fingers look like squat sausages without them. I took off my shoes and they searched inside them. They asked for my wrist splint and saw that there was a metal bar inside it so that went into the envelope. I struggled to get on my shoes as they patted me down, asked me to empty my pockets, and then they patted all around me, my boobs, and like a little clumsy kid I hauled stuff out of my bra, melted twisted protein bars, and they flicked their hands at me as if to say, you can keep those. They let me keep my Advil packet. Then they ushered me into the cell with M. and my fellow dark-haired short activist R., and we were so thankful that there was a blue gym mat laid on top of the metal bench so that we didn't have to sit on cold metal. I sat on one end of the bench, the end near the bars, away from the back wall and the toilet. I guess in retrospect I should have been grateful I got the window seat.

We talked in the cell at first about how we felt about the action, how stunning and well-planned it was, the wall of television cameras, and then afterward I napped for a bit, feeling the cold seep into me through the tights and my jeans, feeling the tiredness of the morning and getting up and all the nervousness in my muscles. M. was a painter, and once we figured out that we both do creative work, she and I talked about the times of the day we like to work, which I think was my question because I like to talk about that. It's been one of the best things in my life to get to determine a schedule that works for me, where creative work has a regular appointed place, where it can grow like a plant. M. told me about her change in painting over the years, from small canvases to huge ones, getting into a certain color palette, for some reason I remember the color blue, then losing 20 years' worth of paintings in Hurricane Sandy because they were all in her basement. What a loss that must have been—I can't even imagine weather taking all that work, but then again I guess that happened to me with technology, all the old Word files on floppy and mini-diskettes in old formats that nothing can open now. I bet you could miss a painting like a person, it's such a visceral record of a moment in time, much more so than a Word file. We branched outward to talk about art, and I said something that hit a nerve with her, that I began to get into visual art once I stopped trying to understand it correctly and instead I just look at what I like, and that your response doesn't have to be complicated.

M. sat up straighter and said that I should try to engage with work even if it doesn't seem pleasing on a surface level, and I got what she was saying especially if I compared it to writing. What I meant but couldn't say is that it was good for me to discover that I could have my own reactions, that I could like and love artwork based on things I couldn't even articulate, that color could be an entry point, and it's okay to pay attention to that. That some things do speak to us on a gut level. I had trouble when I was younger understanding that I had preferences. I guess it is both.

THEN IN THE BROWN dim cell with no window, M. stood up and held a quarter. She raised it and made a mark on the wall with edge of the coin, a metallic line on the beige paint, and she looked at the line, and with a kind of inward satisfaction, she said, "This changes everything."

She got to work on her creation, and it must have taken an hour or more: a kind of fantastical mural with an eyeball in the middle, the long neck of a giraffe near ocean waves, porpoises and a sun and waves radiating outward from the central eye, and it was amazing. In between watching her and talking with her and R., I nodded off and slept, a come-down from all that adrenaline.

The jail was old, with a toilet in the corner with no seat, and in the tiny cell three of us sat on a bench, each with enough room to sit down, and we were in the cell about ten hours altogether. The single thing I took away from it was that it was terrifying even though we were a load of middle-class mostly white women with the additional luxury of flexible time. And I could feel the massive strength of the police, the way the place was tense with potential like a fist, like if they wanted to be mean to you, to hurt you, they could do anything they wanted. I've never seen so clearly my privilege as a white woman, a dozen of us in the police wagon, how we'd crumble if the threat became serious.

SO IT'S NICE TO BE WITH Y. here again outside the courtroom, to get a chance to talk with her, get to know her story, when we are both unhandcuffed, calm, showered. I tell her I'm going to go find the bathroom. I ask at the information desk and go up the massive old staircase made of bluish-gray stone that rises at right angles around a central open area. The stairwell treads have a kind of hardened accretion in the tiny corners and cracks, and on the walls, maybe mop water and mineral deposits hardening into an old gray substance over years and years that look like it has become part of the stone. The steps are so old that they were built for a previous generation of people with more gentle proportions or with a different sense of time.

The whole building feels ancient, reminding me of an old building I ended up in during the one day in my life when I was in Moscow in 1989, when I was in high school on the trip paid for with my Pizza Hut waitressing money. It was a tour of various European capitals at a breakneck budget pace, and we somehow did a lot of drinking with our high school teachers, and we met some local guys who were students at the university and who took us all around, and in the school building there was a bubbled water dispenser with a single glass cup sitting on a shelf in the dispenser that every random stranger used. I ended up kissing one of the guys, who was named Peter and was from Krakow, and then later he asked me to help him emigrate and if he could stay with me, and my mom looked at me like I was possessed by a demon, while my high school boyfriend was understandably wounded. At the time I thought my mom was being unreasonable, as she herself had come here and overstayed a tourist visa, but these are the kind of things that now make me wonder how she survived me, as I must have been exhausting to raise. Now I think how hilarious it is that a school trip let high schoolers—I'd just graduated—wander around in groups in Moscow in 1989, before the wall came down and before cell phones, when Russia was abuzz with Perestroika. We got to see Lenin in his glass case and he looked like wax.

On the second floor of the courthouse, a woman looking harried or tired goes into the District Attorney's office. I follow the walkway around left to the bathroom and wish I had dawdled. I don't want to have to talk to anyone. Why? It's so hard, so much energy to act. But then once I do, I get so much out of talking to people. Pee, wash my hands. Back downstairs, I walk past post-ers in glass cases along the wall describing in multiple languages what to do if you need a lawyer, a gasping fear at what it would feel like to be stuck, to be charged with something inscrutable, to be caught in this net of forms and language and walls.

R., my dark intense twin from the action, shows up next, and she tells us her dad is coming to court because he's so proud of her. That stops me. I exclaim about how wonderful that is, and she seems kind of shy but somehow solid about it, like that is something reliable about her father and his commitments and his love for her. I can't even imagine. My mom knows I'm at court today, is proud of me for having done this, but she didn't ask any questions about it. I think about the decades in which being an activist was a shameful compulsion I had to deal with in my family, and how little I told them about the buses to DC, the actions and work. And now in the Trump era, my mom goes to demonstrations, and she mourns that she gave up her German citizenship and that her chosen country, the United States, has echoes of Nazi Germany.

We sit on the wooden bench and we're so early that we won-der if we are supposed to be somewhere else. "Should we go inside?" one of us says, pointing at the tall wooden door. We stand and one of us opens the door and the three of us go into the courtroom, which is long and high-ceilinged, very cold, with a raised wooden judge's desk at the front. Near the desk is a work area with many desks and lamps and metal slots for file fold-ers, and in front of that area there's a wooden knee-wall with a chain across the opening. We slide into a long wooden pew near the back. Do you just call it a bench when it's not in a church? There's an inscription in metal letters above a plaster rectangle behind the judge's chair. From where I'm sitting, all I can see above the judge's area is the word "Trust," the rest blocked by a hanging fluorescent light.

I joke that I knew R. and I would be here early. "We are the good girls," I say, and Y. says she is too. I think for a second and then I say that I'm good but also very bad, putting my hands out to draw a spectrum in front of me, with "good" and "bad" at the ends of an imaginary number line. It has to do with Catholicism, I think to myself, but Y. was raised in Buddhism and R. was raised Jewish.

"I'm not sure what that is about," I say, "being very concerned with following the rules and then wanting to break them all at once."

R. laughs her soothing dark-eyed laugh and says, "As a therapist, I'd say they're connected." We all laugh. I know that they're connected, but at the same time no one has put it to me that directly before.

So as the conversation continues I'm also watching this little upwelling in my chest: how are they connected? I do have a lot of anger from feeling the pressure to follow the rules, or attending to the rules so closely that you see how senseless they are. I think the shock—ever-present, always renewing—is that the rules are set, but powerful people get to break them. It's something to do with seeing the hypocrisy, or having very high standards for both myself and others and then being crushed by disappointing failure or flagrant violation. Or it all comes from the root of fearing authority, having seen power be abused, knowing I have to toe the line before various capricious gods and hating them all the while. Very few people in authority deserve the power they wield, but then again, that's a closet anarchist talking. That's really all I mean by anarchism. Once I had faith that people could make alternative structures to govern their own worlds. I mean, maybe they could, but these days I also see more of what people are up against, including other people. And now I think the mega-corporation with no constraints is just as dangerous as the state, though really the two are so entwined. Looking forward over the lip of the abyss in the Trump years has made me sort of stunned and foggy, like I'm crouching and ready to take cover rather than to leap into a new world.

Y. says something beautiful about all the activists that have come through this room. I allow myself, momentarily, to feel a part of something bigger. Here in this room, have activists from the Civil Rights movement taken these seats, anti-war activists, or maybe even the 1930s? ACT UP? I think once you're an activist it's very difficult to romanticize activism directly, but the urge to have something sentimental and safe, to be part of a bigger story, makes us all grasp at poses and moments that seem dramatic and comforting. I still don't know whether I'm the wrong person to have been organizing since I've always been so tense and wrecked by the notion that people depended on me. I don't even like to throw parties because I assume no one will come, and that's how an action or event always feels.

Organizing well, taking the inevitable failures, takes a ton of perspective, which I sometimes didn't have in my desperation to reach a goal, even if the real goal was almost always unattainable. In many ways that's the activist's job, to aim for the almost-unreachable and then adapt to the failures that result. I think sometimes about an older Democratic Socialist guy from Columbus, a support person in our leadership board for our Jobs with Justice chapter back in the early 2000s, who would talk me down from anxiety. He called me "Little Pilgrim" once, I think it was part of a quote from some old book I didn't read. Telling me to not worry, to have faith. Sometime in the past few years I saw a tweet from someone about how every organizer he knows had an anxiety disorder, and then I wondered if maybe I wasn't such a terrible aberration after all. What might be called failure happens pretty often. Constantly. We have to always aim for things that aren't possible, aren't "realistic." And then everyone questions your motives. Pictures help, pictures of rallies and meetings and gatherings make the ephemera of moments and effort seem real.

A WOMAN WEARING A BLUE UNIFORM and pushing a wire cart comes down the aisle toward the desk to deliver papers. She stops near where we are sitting in the courtroom benches and tells us that the political people always gather in the hall with their lawyers. We laugh, thank her, and it's so clear with a thousand class markers of our hair, skin, clothes, demeanor that we are not here alone, that this is not our "place," that we have done something that is protected by the numbers of people who did it but also by who we are in society. So we get up to go out back into the waiting area, and as Y. gets up, she drops her huge bulky coat, and I carry it out for her, a thick weight over my arm. She's not overly apologetic or flustered, which is beautiful. She's also not clueless and entitled, either. I wonder if she's had to work hard over the years to not apologize for being a person and taking up space as a woman. Everything I do is an "I'm sorry," a bow to the crushing power of gossip and judgment for a woman, how "being a bitch" can get you cut off from social sustenance—or at least that is what my body believes. So I will help make a massive snarl of traffic in Times Square but will also apologize when I am sitting in a place that is blocking you from where you want to get to, even if I'm just sitting and was there before you arrived.

We sit back outside in the waiting area on the wooden pews that line the square-shaped lobby with big square plaster pillars that go up to the ceiling and a floor that is maybe marble. Y. tells us she's working on staging an adaptation of a Tennessee Williams play about incarceration, replacing the men characters with women to see if it works. That makes me think about how often the work that's commonly known and taught from past eras' authors isn't the political stuff, how the author's connection to social movements isn't known, perpetuating the false impression that authors weren't deeply engaged in politics. I say that I'm researching Mark Twain for something I'm writing, how he lost all his money investing in a typewriter prototype and his wife was sick so he went over to Europe in the 1890s and became an anti-imperialist, but how some critics today describe that period as when he lost his sense of humor, as if that was a personal failing during a period when his wife and then a daughter died, and later another daughter. As if amusement was his only function. The house he built in upstate Connecticut in the years before he died was called Stormfield, which is a beautiful word that I connect to as a fellow Midwesterner. One of the singular things I miss about my home landscape is watching a huge storm roll up above the flat earth, the crashing rain that smells of minerals. I don't say any of this.

R. is working on a dissertation about psychotropic (I think?) drugs, how micro-dosing of LSD and mushrooms has been shown to work in treating depression and other disorders, how there's an institute in Amsterdam she went to do research with. That reminds me of that guy and that girl who were at the Zen Center where I stayed during the meditation retreat, a quiet cold place in November 2018 when I got my fill of silence, and I haven't been meditating enough since. Anyway those two people at the center were really into drugs as a way to "see" things and know yourself and get over traumatic issues. My private reaction to that is that my head contains all the amusement and weirdness I need, I have no desire to trip. This comes from seeing a lot of alcohol abuse and, too, from a long fear of fucking up my brain, the organ that was my ticket out of New Lenox, Illinois.

Also does tripping really count as processing emotions, or is it just taking a kind of shortcut around them? But then again I have been in therapy for so long, and some of these patterns and mental habits are sticky, like maybe you do need to jolt yourself into a new reality when nothing else works. But also when I was in college in Minnesota I saw a guy on mushrooms in a dorm run around and around screaming that he was going to die because his heart was going to explode, and then the ambulance took him away, and I remember my ex-boyfriend on acid stroking the lawn and telling me how amazing it felt. I could get to that state all on my own, and it was way cheaper just to be me. But on the other hand, I've been medicated on and off since college, almost thirty years, but with Zoloft, and how different is that than micro-dosing, and also I have done EMDR for PTSD and it worked really really well. So what do I know.

I don't say any of that because I don't want to come off as judgmental, and I think anything that treats mental health issues is one hundred percent awesome because depression, having been there, is terrifying, like drowning in pig souse or gray gelatin. I'm always about two paces away from it, and I recognize that I need to be less afraid of it because it's a part of the place I live. Maybe admitting that will let me grasp something about myself and my life. Like yeah, my property does have a sinkhole, so just put a fence around it and plant things. So who am I to judge. But I also thought it was sad in a way that those young people in Colorado were looking for peak experiences and sitting in sweat lodges and kind of using rituals that are not from their culture, when the real meat of life is not the peaks, it's learning to be bored and to be comfortable with the meat you've got to work with, but then again, my meat's on Zoloft, so who can say. Still there was something wild in their eyes as if they'd "discovered" something that normal fearful straitlaced people just didn't get, and they were proud to be in on the secret. Y. tells R. that there are small Burning Man festivals that take place in every state, which might be an interesting way to connect with people interested in her topic. Who knew?

I cannot even imagine a Connecticut Burning Man, that would be kind of hilarious, like everything matchy-matchy and Vineyard Vines but also raging on drugs, and Burning Man makes me think of my sister, who lived in the southwest and likes music festivals and was involved with them for part of her career. I don't know if Burning Man is her scene, but she loves music and there are lots of bands there, I guess? I just always imagine it as being my vision of pure hell: no one wearing underwear, everyone dirty but also very beautiful and fashionable, wandering around covered in glitter in a recreational catastrophe of their own making, probably with no decent coffee or books anywhere. I guess I'm judgmental of the whole "substance" route, because it has hurt me. I loved someone with a drug problem, which isn't a personality flaw, just a thing. I've got depression and anxiety, and I'm in constant recovery from an addiction to sad stories and emergencies.

I'll admit, though, what has really hurt me was not admitting what I wanted, trying to tolerate behavior that made me uncomfortable and telling myself I was uptight, gaslighting myself into "relaxing" because I wanted to be cool, bad, normal. I wore myself down to a nub to fight for some abstract notion of love. I could have left, but instead I made it about loyalty and ethics rather than about my own comfort and safety. I also found a kind of thin wisp of steam to continue or maybe the reason to continue from the images of my suffering Catholic foremothers, their visions of Saint Lucy with her eyes on her plate. The epigenetics of stigmata.

But that's not "looking for a fixer-up," as if the tendency to help were a personality flaw. We ambulance-people have often had someone in our past who needed saving, whose un-savedness shaped our deepest templates, carved our genes and muscles and worries and days into the quest to save. It's not stupidity, it's humans adapting to the conditions in which they were born, an unavoidable universal. We talk about it and celebrate it a lot less than the recovery from addiction, probably because of the sexism that adheres to the stereotyped notion that addicts are men and their wives are the nagging shrews, but our half's recovery is also noble and vital. How to refind one's self. Well, it's really how to find one's self for the first time. And so I creep slowly into myself.

WHAT I LIKE. WHAT I WANT. Sometimes I'm tempted as a reminder to start a list, so I remember: cobblestones, used bookstores, my Dyson vacuum cleaner because it's easy to fix and take apart, the smell before rain as well as the smell after (if petrichor is the smell after, what is the smell before? It should be something like electrichor.) I like quiet and being alone and time to think and big paintings with indigo splotches and girls with odd haircuts. There should have been an assembly in high school for nerds where they tell you to notice what you like, go toward what makes you feel safe and good and what matters to you. But then again, that was the 1980s in the Midwest and there are many reasons why no one wanted high school girls to absorb that message. The most punk rock thing ever is admitting what you like. And I like ruined places, anything the world has put its stamp on, anyplace worn and wild. I like beads and making art and going to museums and movies.

The funny thing is that now I have a medical marijuana card for my rheumatoid arthritis. I did mushrooms at a Grateful Dead show in Illinois, and I am told I laughed for eight hours straight. All I remember is being annoyed by the music, somehow buying a $35 T-shirt (and this was in the 1990s), and with all the T-shirts for sale in acres of parking lot I was uncool enough to buy the "official" one, and then because it was raining we watched people slide on the mud down the lawn of the arena. I've done some things that I can't even remember having fun doing.

TWO MORE PEOPLE come into the courtroom waiting area, a man and a woman who seem to be a couple, and I don't remember them from that day, but we all smile and say hi. We recognize each other because we're white and unlined, because we haven't smoked many cigarettes and have had access to good food and semi-regular healthcare and so it's hard to place our ages, the white East Coast college-educated people who feel such a stake in the world that they think they can save it, the people who feel entitled enough to stop traffic with a neon green boat. The man and the woman are wearing black windbreakers, all the brand names and outdoorsy styles that I first encountered in college. I was so disoriented when I got to campus, immediately understanding that everything about me was wrong. On the lawns and in the dorms I saw a new world, a crowd of people who did not shop at Kmart for basics and at the Limited when they wanted to be fancy, people who lived in the kind of hiking clothes I thought were just for professionals climbing Mount Everest. My first time hiking in college I had to borrow an old frame backpack from a friend in my dorm and a pair of old tan work boots that I fell in love with because they were sturdy and comfortable. My friend Topher went on that hike, so driven into hippiedom that he thought he could take a multi-day hike through mountains in the rainy Boundary Waters of Minnesota in Birkenstocks and he ripped his feet right open and then something happened to him later, he got into girls and drugs, and now he's dead.

R. tells me about an upcoming Black Friday action. It sounds amazing and right up my alley: they plan to do meditation right in the middle of the street as the shoppers visit New York. I look into the Signal messages on my phone to find the online sign-up form and sign up. More people are arriving now from our action, and an older nervous man with curly white-gray hair and glasses sits down next to me. He was arrested by the same officer that R. and I were, and I tell him about the Black Friday action. He seems to imply that he has trouble with finding things on the internet, so I tell him I can email him the link, so he tells me his email and I send it to him.

R. says she's surprised I didn't know about the upcoming action, she thought I'd be totally into it, but I tell her that the app, Signal, is overwhelming to me; I'm on several lists and I see the alerts. They all show up as text messages so I have about 200 unread ones, and I like to see them but I just can't keep track. Part of me, a secret part, knows that I can't keep engaged regularly like this, that I don't have the mental or physical energy with a job and a kid and my health and my local activism and my writing. I do say that the train time into the city, an hour and a half each way, makes it kind of not work on a regular basis with my life, and so someone helps me look up the Connecticut XR branch. My inbox, to be honest, is an utter mess, and I'm just grateful that Gmail does the sorting, and even so I miss a lot of stuff. I miss emails that contain requests and people asking me for favors, and then I reply to them all at once. And then the work email, messages on social media.

I am so excited about the meditation action but it turns out that I will end up not going because at that time in the semester I will be too worn out. It's hard to explain, and I think my non-teaching friends with more regular schedules don't get it, but the work and the scheduling never stops, all the face-to-face stuff and students who need you to be a whole feeling person, present, in your interactions, and you need to encourage them and mean it. Then evenings and weekends are for grading and emailing and lesson planning, so for the course of the semester, at least for me, the focus changes to how I can survive, how I can get it all done. I think it's because I have a compulsion to do everything as well as I can, an assumption that even after all this time that I'm going to mess up and expose myself as a fraud and fail my students, plus the autoimmune stuff means that I'm often pushed beyond my capacity in terms of the length of the days and the level of work. Thankfully now I can choose to skip meetings and pull back when I need to. For me there's a constant feeling, too, of faking at being a professor when I always feel like the person I am, at my core, won't pass in that role. And so I have to be extra aware and amped up to build the hologram of seeming professional or right.

Somehow I feel less driven to keep up with it all these days, post tenure, and also secretly the getting arrested itself exhausted me on such a deep bodily level that I don't know if I'll make myself do that again. When I was in jail, at a certain point, cold and bone exhausted, I told myself that once was enough.

But even so, getting arrested was easier physically than the thing that is supposed to be the quintessential form of activism, the long protest march, either in DC or anywhere else. I've done a bunch of them since the first one in college, which I think was against "Hunger and Homelessness." That was a term in the 1980s when liberal people couldn't quite get up to saying "Poverty and Capitalism and Reaganomics" or the organizers were trying to be nonconfrontational. I remember trying to grasp the causes of poverty as a college freshman, a kind of vagueness in a lecture hall, a panel discussion, but then I just left with kind of a blank feeling because we were talking about the problem without a context. It turned out the answers were very big: exploitation, history, capitalism. Without those words and cause-and-effect, the world was very mysterious. Not understanding is not a crime, just a lack of information.

But the bus rides to big marches, the shuffle-march for miles, the standing: my body can't handle that anymore, which is something that able-bodied people don't get, and they don't understand that there are disabled people all around them, people not in wheelchairs but still disabled. After the action, someone tweeted about the XR protests being inaccessible to disabled people. I replied that, yes, this is true, depending on the disability, but also that sitting down in Times Square and getting arrested and sitting in jail for ten hours was easier on my disabled body than an all-day march, or a multi-day trip to DC for a march. And then I erased the tweet.

There was a woman in my group of arrestees who had one arm without a hand, just a narrowed and shortened stump, how funny she was, long hair, olive skin, wide-legged plaid pants and a roguish smile. She and R. and I went to the bathroom in Bryant Park before the action, hopped up on adrenaline and excited, a gaggle of girls headed to pee and laughing like at a grade-school field trip to the zoo. And then she was laughing later as the police lined us up because handcuffs require two hands to work, and the policemen looked down at her stump and then up at each other, confronted with a new engineering problem. They ended up using a pair of metal handcuffs around her one hand and looping the other end of the cuffs around her belt loop.

R. gets up when M., our other cellmate who drew with the quarter, arrives, and we hug. M.'s been in Venice—no, I thought she was in Venice but it's all flooded, higher than even what Venice itself was built for as a city of water. Now water is sweeping up into fantastic old buildings and plazas and churches, all the ancient stone and paintings and treasures. M. was in Madrid, talked to separatists there. She says she's in a weird headspace because she was spending time with the work of Goya. She retired early after doing graphic design for a union for a long time. Her partner is also an artist and they happened to buy a building in New York when it was cheap and now they are in a lucky pocket of income where they can do what they want.

WHEN WE WERE IN THE CELL we each imagined whether our spouses would get arrested, and for each of them, it was a "no way." I think Cliff might, for some cause he felt strongly about, as he's spoken at demonstrations before, but it would have to be the right cause and he'd have to feel personally connected. I remember him speaking at what they called Sweetheart Circle at GSU, the rally against the budget cuts, when he was on the news giving a bold and rip-roaring speech. For some reason that day he had a cutout of the Cat in the Hat from Dr. Seuss in his shirt pocket, so I have a picture of him holding it with its striped red and white hat and grinning. Maybe it was from his little cousin or maybe Ivan? Kids were supposed to give or send these cutouts to people and then collect photos of where the cat cutouts journeyed in the world, so maybe that was the only one that ended up on TV news at a protest. The news clip with Cliff giving a speech apparently got his adjunct contract mysteriously not renewed, because if there's one thing part-timers don't have, it's academic freedom or freedom of speech. That began our slow detachment from Georgia. He taught a class at a college in Savannah, volunteered at Ivan's school in the first-grade classroom, and then had to go on unemployment. The Obama economic recovery program helped us stay afloat. And then I was on the job market, no ability to really choose, just needed the first job that was offered, which was how I ended up in Connecticut.

During that conversation in the cell, R. talked about her research. Then the red-haired woman in the next cell who had told me the rumor about Rikers started singing and led us in all kind of songs with a great strong deep voice. She sang silly song about a mango and other fruits in the form of a round, which she somehow coordinated us to do even though we couldn't see each other in the row of cells, and then people started us on every other song they could think of, and at first I didn't sing but after a while I did. Then someone passed a request down from one cell to another that we have some quiet time, which I understood. Our nerves were all a little frayed. We didn't know what time it was. A guard came by and asked if we wanted water, so we each gratefully took a plastic cup of water and I swallowed my Advil. I had taken some in the morning too, which I was consistently glad about throughout the day. Then we got a refill of water. Then later a woman came by with a huge clear garbage bag filled with cheese sandwiches on wheat bread, and I took one because I was hungry, thinking I might pick off the cheese, but it was stuck to the bread, and I couldn't really stomach it. R. passed gum to me and I chewed and sucked on one piece of gum, then another. Then I ate a melted messy protein bar, opening up the wrapper to pick out the chunks of melted chocolate and a fibrous substance like the inside of a Butterfinger bar. Butterfinger is a candy bar I am positive I never purchased in my life, what a weird, weird food that for some reason reminds me of fiberglass, but somehow they were always in our house at Halloween, maybe because my dad liked them, in the big bowl of candy near the door. The bowl was aluminum printed with a wood pattern, and we also used it to make stuffing at Thanksgiving. My dad had won it in a contest in the 1970s where you could enter ideas for what to do with aluminum, and he had some idea related, I think, to shielding for the nuclear sources used to check on the safety of X-ray equipment in hospitals, which was his job.

At some point in the cell we were talking about our families, and I told R. and M. about a close person in my life who did some months in jail for what ended up being a felony, an error in a young life, a chunk of time that I think traumatized this person and added another layer of difficulty on top of others. I told R. and M. that being here gave me a sliver of a sense about what it must have been like for that person. Of course I couldn't know. I don't suddenly understand that experience, but at least now I have a grain of sand-sized way in. Hearing the word "felon" has always stung me, the personal knowledge of this stigma and all the ways it limits a life, limits job opportunities and credit and voting, which adheres only to some crimes, a smashed window, and not to larger crimes like defrauding a company, a nation.

Somehow my comment about my loved one being in jail kind of killed our conversation in the cell and marked a pause I felt in my chest. R. and M. looked at me and didn't have any experience to relate, and even though I know they didn't think it, I half-wondered if they had an initial impulse that I was gross or low-class, not who they thought, by association. Somehow you can feel these tides beneath the surface in a conversation, and I felt dirty and lumpy, ragged and wrong. It's nothing that they did, and maybe I was imagining that and they weren't thinking that at all. Or maybe it was something too intimate to share? But that wasn't really an intimate thing. It just ended up making me feel odd, because I came from a different kind of family than either of them came from. In the quiet of the cell I spun into a tiny world of wrongness like a spiral down into myself, the ungainly Midwestern girl who is awkward and bought her jeans at Kmart, the one who didn't even understand into her twenties that she had blackheads or should have bought a separate soap to wash her face. This is an exaggeration of my teenage or college years, but I suppose everyone has holes inside them that they fall into. Then comes that feeling that I get sometimes, that I have offered a story that I shouldn't have offered, but sometimes when I do that, it's a feeling of complete safety and peace and someone responds with an honest connection.

R. and I tried to sleep with our heads resting on our pulled-up knees, and M. scratched her painting. I felt my achy bones, stood up to stretch, leaned down to touch the floor, then moved my torso over one leg and another, then stood back up and stretched backward in an arch. Then I sat back down, tucked my head into my knees to make darkness and sleep. At some point during the hours, I watched my inner white lady get irate/panic/ want to control the outcome of this, like, "Excuse me can I speak to the manager? Do you not know how to efficiently run a jail? Couldn't you process us and let us go?" Then irrationally I worried I'd never get out, and I saw what a gulf, a massive unbridgeable gulf, separated me from those who have been rightly or wrongly convicted of crimes and truly imprisoned. I watched the itchiness of my soul, all the ways I flung around that little squishy octopus of my ego, rapping on all the doors, lodging complaints and things I like and don't like. I guess that would have to be the second high school assembly after "Find what you like." It would be called "Stop worrying about what you like." Or "Don't make a religion out of it."

I thought about the two rows of white women handcuffed in the back of a police wagon, and I thought maybe that every white woman should have to have that experience, not to be a fluffy peacock but just have to be locked in a van as part of a load of white women, but then after thinking it through for two seconds I realized how quickly white women would misconstrue and ruin any value in the experience. There'd be wine glasses and T-shirts with terrible puns and in horrible looping script, there'd be whole Etsy stores devoted to the best supplies for jail, it would just turn in on itself like white woman origami. The question of how to call in white women, the 53% who voted for Trump, that daunting figure that I find not surprising at all, but Pew Research Center later said it was only 45%, but still, and how so many of the white women I knew and grew up with would laugh in my face if I tried to bring up racism or Trump, how deeply ingrained it all is in the rough ridges like tire tracks in that place. I know, too, that even fanning out my awareness of white womanhood is a very white-woman thing to do. The Matryoshka doll of white womanhood. People expect almost nothing of white guys, so on one level, anything human they do is gravy, until you're one of those horrific dudes so proud of themselves. White women hold and reproduce the terrible essence of America.

Then a guard appeared with keys and they began taking out the people who had been glued or chained to the boat during the action, one by one, to notify them that they were receiving higher charges. And then one by one they brought them back. Then hours passed, hours where we sat, talked, and at one point I played rock paper scissors with the redhead from the next cell, even though I couldn't see her, we were each waggling our fists out into the hallway, but I got tired of that pretty quickly. Then more worrying about what time it was, trying to meditate and watch my brain, thinking about the next day since I actually had to go and teach, hoping I didn't miss the last train.

Then finally they started, after hours more, to retrieve people randomly from various cells to release them. M. had gotten arrested before and told us that our arresting officer would need to come get us in order for us to go free. But it had been so long, what if he'd gone home? We tried to remember his name from his name tag—it had G's in it. We stood at the bars and looked out for any movement down the hall through a window in the door. We listened for the clank of keys, or any clomping sounds or movement or noise beyond the closed door. There were posters on the wall opposite the cell in English and Spanish saying that we had a right to food and water, and that if we were here for over 24 hours we should ask someone to check into our case. I thought about what that must be like: not understanding what those signs mean, or asking someone in a way that makes them angry at you, or having a cop decide to beat the hell out of you for no reason, or asking if someone will check on your case and then never getting an answer, waiting for time to maybe pass and maybe not, sitting with only the air in the cell and trying to imagine what your options might be.

The bars were covered in drips of dried goopy tan-brown paint, as if they'd been hastily painted over and over. There was a horizontal shelf at about hip height set into in the bars, a rectangle where things could be passed through, and a doorplate in the door with a lock and keyhole in it. This was not an electrified jail, it was an old-school completely mechanical cell opened with a brown-greenish metal key. We listened for the clang-slam of doors, the smash of keys. Finally almost the whole row of cells was empty, and we were still there, and every time an officer came in to call out a last name, we all stood at the bars. There was a sort of a fantasy—similar to waiting in line at a cash register or coffeeshop where nothing seems to be happening—that if I made a certain kind of piercing eye contact, I might have been able to awaken some urgency or produce a different outcome. Such an outrageous assumption, such a kind of low-key bitchiness, one that comes as an edge in me right before I surrender to hopelessness. And on the other hand: asking and complaining is also important, as long as you're not taking other people down. If you don't say something, the world will run right over you. And then finally a woman came up and unlocked our door as she called our names, and clank-swing, the door was open, and we walked out into the hallway, and the other women remaining in the cells cheered as we had cheered for everyone else who was getting out.

We lined up near the door where we came in along the brown filing cabinets—what must even be inside the files, from what decade?—and one by one, we got our manila folders, and we stuffed our pockets with our stuff. I had forgotten about all of these objects, my gray semi-transparent scarf, my wrist splint that I stuffed in my pocket. I was achy and clumsy. We were nudged and directed about where to go next. We walked past a big glassed-in area with a bunch of old wooden seats, like a fishbowl, but from the 1940s. That's where the men were, held all together. We heard about this in training, that the men organize the whole experience in that glass cell, lead each other in yoga and discussions, that they do sharing and talking about activism and meditations where you stare into each other's eyes and training on the basics of XR. I'm so glad I didn't have to live through hours of that. The room was right opposite the long wooden intake desk, I guess so the police could keep an eye on who was inside, so maybe that's what they call the drunk tank, and there was a clock, and I saw it was 10 p.m. As an officer ushered us toward the desk on our left, with police milling around, C. started talking to the officer about the sea levels rising, and her voice got louder, she was starting some kind of intense discussion with this cop, trying to persuade him, and yes she was saying all true things, like if we didn't do something now, we really were all going to die, and yes, it was big oil paying off politicians for their silence, and we said, "Stop, stop. It's enough."

I don't know why I felt uncomfortable with her pressing the cop but I also felt irrationally cranky and afraid, like any deviation from the script would send us into another eddying bureaucratic waiting room, like if we made them mad, they could take more hours. We were led up to the desk, three at a time, and we were handed pens to fill out name and address on a form that would tell us where to go for court and what our charge was. I filled something out wrong, put the time in the date place, and an officer pointed where I had to scratch something out and change it. I took the form. We moved our bodies this way and that in the low-ceilinged place, clutching our papers, so attuned to any subtle motions of the cops' hands and torsos and eyes, directing and pointing us through one door, then another, then a heavy metal door, and then the arresting officer guy, who clearly despised us from the pits of his eyes, stood and pointed outward. And we were out, through the yard, past the chain-link gate and that closed hut-thing with the metal roof and the parked wagons, into a parking lot lit with overhead lights, into the wind and the cold.

It was raining and blowing and dark, and our embed D. was standing beneath a streetlight on a street corner opposite the alley. He had waited all day for us as part of the jail support team, standing with his backpack full of our stuff. His poncho billowed in the wind and rain like a sail, and he handed us our phones and our Ziploc bags filled with our keys and stuff, and we hugged him.

After a quick check-in, he sent us up a hill through an alley and then around a corner to where jail support was located. R. and I hurried; we were both intent on getting onto a train and getting home home home. We walked uphill in a dark street, and I had no idea where we were going, but R. had absorbed more information than I had. We reached a corner and turned left, heading near an overhang or some scaffolding, maybe the set-back entrance to an apartment building next to a row of closed shops, and there was jail support in a circle of light. As we approached there were smiles and people let forth a kind of hoarse whisper-cheer, it was a large crowd, someone explained that there was a noise complaint so they had to be quiet. There were long tables of food, Tupperware containers of hummus and dips and paper plates, rectangle aluminum pans filled with things to eat, but even though I was probably hungry I didn't want to stop for a second, R. and I seemed to have agreed upon this wordlessly. We were rushed, dazed, uncomfortable, so tired and wanting the subway, where is the subway.

We were ushered past the food to a man in a suit, a lawyer who was clearly also an anarchist (these things seem contradictory but are not at all) because his suit was a wrinkled mess, and I got the sense, as I had absorbed over decades with dear activists, that the suit was never not a wrinkled mess, even in court.

And maybe he tried to make the suit nice at one point, but he was someone like me, someone who was always distracted by thoughts of strategy and tactics and coffee and daydreams and grand schemes and so was always ripping his clothing and spilling things on himself and therefore less attentive to dry cleaning. His hair, also, had that anarchist semi-unwashed look, which was also fine. And yet he also exuded complete competence, like the kind of competence you would want on your apocalypse team, which also might seem like a contradiction with being an anarchist, but that's only if you don't know any social ecologist/syndicalist/collective-oriented anarchists. They are people who are so clear about stepping up and doing the next right thing, working with whatever is at hand, and also not the subset of lefties on Twitter who seem to hate everyone.

I'm writing this, now, as the coronavirus crisis escalates in March 2020 and there are anarchists in a mutual aid group sharing plans about how to use a 3D printer to print intubation supplies. Anyway I'm only comfortable writing about my love of anarchists now that I'm a full professor, which is both understandable and like the biggest statement of me being a sellout ever. But at the SAME time, my anarchists are not the mean mocking kinds, they're very loving and they don't care what you choose for work, because we are all imperfect.

Anyway, the lawyer who looks like he slept in his suit—and to be fair, he had also had a very long day—asked us if he could take a picture of the forms we were holding with the court date written on it, because XR kept track of all this information to help guide us through the legal process. He put our sheets down on a folding table, one after the other, and took a photo with his phone. We thanked him profusely. We asked someone about the way to the subway, and again I think R. retained more than me. Still, we walked a bit in the direction we were supposed to go but then we were both confused. Separately we both used Google maps to look at the route, standing in the dark looking at our almost-dead phones. R. saw that there were two possible routes, but the signal was weak and our maps kept freezing. One route that showed up on my screen was a dotted line that led under a highway overpass, a jog we had to take that was left and then straight again, and then somehow we arrived in the wind and the spitting drizzle at the subway entrance, which felt vacant and tiled and fluorescent as we walked down the cement steps, and she knew the subway and had to take one train and I was supposed to take another. We hugged and dashed. I found the right train to Grand Central, and it slid in before long, and I felt like I always feel on public transportation, an extra thrill that something greater than myself was functioning so powerfully.

Public transportation is like one form of my higher power, religion and politics combined. Anyway, I was proud to know I was headed to where I wanted to go. Then it turned out I would not miss the last Metro North home, which I'd worried about, and I had put a change of clothes in my van at the train station in Connecticut just in case I had to crash with someone in the city and then get the morning train, change, and go teach. But that night I would get to sleep in my own bed. I had enough cash in the zip pocket at the back of my phone for a bag of air-pop popcorn chips and an orange juice in the convenience store— still open!—in Grand Central. I felt, without my credit cards and keys, with a phone number in permanent marker scrawled on my arm, with so many layers of clothing both sweaty and cold at the same time, like I was sneaking somewhere where I was not technically allowed. But here I was still allowed to use money and buy things, and then I found the next train, waiting by the track with the glowing red bulbs that spelled NEW HAVEN, and it chuffed and pulled away from the station, and it moved and stopped and moved, leaving jail behind, and I got out at the stop where I'd parked my van, and I was home by 1 a.m.

NOW, SITTING ON A BENCH waiting for court as people gather, I ask M., who drew with a quarter on the wall, questions about Spain. I tell her that I would get to go to the South of France for a conference on James Baldwin the next summer, and saying that, I feel like the most ridiculous of a cliché of an academic, that I as a white woman get to go talk on a panel and get part of my travel paid to go think about Baldwin (of course, this is pre-COVID-19, so we don't yet know that will all be canceled). I am living a life arbitrarily denied to 75 percent of the academics in my position who are teaching and writing and mentoring students but who didn't have the good fortune and random luck to get a full-time position.

When I taught in Georgia, I remember childless academics asking me whether I knew a certain neighborhood in Italy, as if everyone did, and I'd never been to Italy. But what was so jarring was the expectation, or the assumption, that Italy was where we all went, when I was a single mom hauling myself out of an extended period of hard times. But now in retrospect I watch myself trying to draw the slightest distinctions I can, holding myself at a distance so I don't have to really understand what I have access to. The trip to the conference would be my first time really cashing in on the academic scheme of getting a paper accepted to an international conference during the summer so that you can also get a vacation out of it. We had planned, before COVID, on making it a family trip, taking my son and my mom and a cousin.

I wonder how different I seem to M. In this moment it feels like I am not the woman in front of her who had confessed that her family member had been in jail. This is the life of eyeliner and credit cards and academia. So we can talk and hear in a new way outside of the cell, and then we get into talking about Baldwin, what I plan to talk about at the conference that would eventually be canceled. I feel the spatial brightness of ideas, and I began to talk with my hands, because the shape of essays is what I like, their three-dimensional presence in my mind's eye. I am now reading a book on gestures and how they are a language, how they might have enabled and still enable abstract thought. I cannot think without shaping the air in front of me. So with the confidence of eyeliner and credit cards, I shape the air in that courtroom waiting room in lower Manhattan.

In front of me in the air is sort of a landscape of the essay, and this is what the author Barbara Tversky of *Mind in Motion: How Action Shapes Thought* describes, that there's a sort of working grid in our brains that we use over and over like an Etch A Sketch to map out gesture, or at least that's what I understood of it. She writes, "When people are asked to describe or explain spatial relationships while sitting on their hands, they have trouble speaking. They can't find words."

I talk about what Baldwin does with his language and ideas, which to me are much more complex than simply relaying a story or even reflecting on the meaning of experiences. His modulation, his ability to move between voices, and to hit a kind of low gravely spinal point, and then to work up to a kind of church-like crescendo of swooping sentences that call forth a human's sense of possibility and spirit and best self—all that is in his essays, and from what I've experienced in reading essays, he is rare in that regard. I believe he is an opera-and-blues singer of the essay. She tells me that she had read Baldwin's novels all at once and got so sad, and a friend said, of course. But she didn't know much about his nonfiction.

So as I talk to M., I feel as a physical experience that kind of twirling spiritual flight Baldwin makes from a level landscape that he clears with words. I make a sort of sweep and parenthesis with my hands, and then a kind of bringing upward, both hands in a goblet shape, a force to the sky, an offering. I say, *Oh the nonfiction is . . . it's so*—I open my hands—*it's so big.* I tell her there's a complete collection of his work that came out a few years ago, and I read all of it at once, lived inside it. I picture the physical weight of the collection, edited by Toni Morrison, with the slim stripe of red, white, and blue on a black cover, with the title in script, *Baldwin,* above it, and his picture, a black and white of him leaning on one elbow holding a cigarette and looking off toward one side, as if in knowing contemplation of some bullshit coming out of someone's mouth. His voice is like fierce compassion, I say, though I don't know if he would have described it that way.

I had written before about the question of why Baldwin is not taught enough in the K–12 classroom, and therefore not enough in the college classroom, how he's in danger of being relegated to 1960s political writers as a historical curiosity, his sophisticated language and subject matter. How to save his work in the public consciousness in the face of the Common Core, the public curriculum revamp that focused on nonfiction as historical documentation rather than as literature. I tell her I'll email her some good Baldwin essays and quotes, because I have a page of them on my blog from when I got obsessed, and random schoolkids sometimes find the blog page and write little thank you notes. She tells me that she might want to use a Baldwin essay as a reading for XR, because the group as a whole is very white and grappling with that, what it means and how to build beyond that or critically examine the causes.

XR has partnered with Movimiento Cosecha, part of the immigrant rights movement in the US and with the same kind of decentralized structure as XR. But XR also needs to grapple with the inherent white privilege of voluntarily being arrested, and also to look at the culture within itself, to understand how it perpetuates itself as a majority white group. It might be, like so many activist groups, that there's so much emphasis on how much you can give, how much time you can contribute, and that those with the most free or flexible time end up determining a de facto core and culture. A thrown-together or ad-hoc organizational structure usually pays less attention to sustaining community activities and offering a range of levels and ways to get involved, to lead, and make decisions. If you are working and/or parenting and have schedule constraints, it's very difficult to plug in. I feel that too. Plus sometimes in activism we treat each other like construction materials, which is not conducive to building trust, especially among people who have no prior personal connection to each other. XR will, the next spring, use its network to support Black Lives Matter, but then the relationship will fray, and I find this completely predictable, as white activist culture is hampered by patterns that often end up causing harm. Somehow a sense of urgency leads many white activists to a kind of aggression, a thinking that we don't have time to listen or breathe, when that is when it is most needed.

M. remembers me mentioning in the cell that my husband and I took our son and his cousin and my mom on a massive hilarious road trip through Germany in 2018 so my son could finally meet his relatives for the first time. Amazing that my mom and I had never traveled through Europe together as tourists.

M. says, *This time you won't be able to speak the language if you go to France.* I tell her how I'm a little daunted by planning a trip through France and northern Italy where my husband's extended family comes from, but my mom doesn't seem daunted at all, she's enthusiastic and loves planning itineraries, she just dives in. It's hard to describe my mom to strangers, but with this, too, I tend to use my whole body and face and hands in describing her, because she's a little fireplug of a woman. I always say she should be leading armies or a country, but also that she would be terrible at that because it would stress her out. She has always been so happy and up for any adventure. The other night after I shared a glowing picture of her on Facebook, I said to Cliff, "She's got such an intense amazing mixture of utter joy and doom. I've never seen anything like it anywhere." Then I paused, realizing. "Oh," I said, "except . . ." And then we both laughed, because: me.

SOMEHOW M. AND I get back into talking about art, and I tell her how I teach, somehow explaining how my priorities in the classroom come from Buddhism and risk. I grade my students not based on perfection for their final projects but on whether they're able to let go of a final polished product and instead step back from it and do something else to it, take it apart and make something new with the pieces. I am most comfortable describing these things around visual artists, who seem to be completely open to connections like this and who have been less overtaken by our need as English teachers to describe everything in terms of the dominant language, which has shifted rightward toward measurement and goals and outcomes as the humanities gets stepped on over and over.

Her face lights up because she understands risk, how central it is. I have known this on some level about visual artists, but more and more now that I'm older I see how their open thinking is even more free than most writers I know, and why I so much always need visual art in my life. When I tell her these things, sitting in the gathering of people in the lobby, I sense a solid attention, almost as if, for a moment, I am inside her head as she looks at a painting in process, as if my telling her this is connecting to her experience of color and the wet texture of paint.

I tell her about the obsession notebook, an assignment I was first given in grad school by the writer Bill Roorbach, when I was a journalism grad student. I had stumbled into a fellowship for mid-career reporters after a coworker at a magazine told me to apply, and that was how I learned that at a state school someone might pay me to go to grad school, and then all the reporters were talking about this creative nonfiction class in the English department, which blew the roof right off my understanding of nonfiction, and I fell hard in love.

I didn't even do the obsession notebook assignment correctly. I forgot about it, which was particularly terrible because I had gotten into the class through Bill making a special allowance for me. During the week it was due, we went to DC for the journalism program, and we had tours and met the staff of the *Washing-*

ton Post and I didn't write enough in my notebook. I was staying in a hotel room I didn't have to share, and I was kind of freaking out that someone had paid for the nicest hotel I'd ever stayed in. I remember marble counters in the bathroom, and it was cold, snow drifts everywhere outside on the streets of DC and a bitter wind. I completed the little notebook later that spring, after spring break. I used the pages to vent about the stress of being sent to collections for healthcare bills. After the DC trip, I went to Chicago to do some reporting for a story on working conditions in the mental health industry in Illinois for my journalism thesis, and while I was there and out of state I found that the cranberry juice wasn't enough to treat a kidney infection, so I was hospitalized at Silver Cross, where they saved my life.

Avoiding the phone calls from Neil my collections agent, I barfed my anxiety into that little notebook, which turned into a book idea. And now I assign my undergraduates this assignment, only I give them ten days, and what I love SO MUCH is that whenever I take these packages of notebooks from my tote bag and prepare to hand them out, there's always the tiniest gasp of pleasure from the class: presents. They love the little notebooks. Students in all kinds of majors have emailed me to tell me that at terrible or just stuck times in their lives, they've bought one of the notebooks at a drugstore and dumped everything into it, and that it's helped. There's something bracing and clean about the rush of writing, and the sense of accomplishment afterward.

A WOMAN WHOSE NAME I forget, the one who had the farm in Vermont and was also in our police wagon, is sitting on the wooden bench on the other side of M., and she's knitting with a cool kind of multi-colored German wool, a pattern with nibs and bubbles. I lean over to compliment her on it and she says she's knitting a sweater for her grandchild. She's got a nice open face, blue eyes and bangs going gray. I also compliment her on the XR buttons on her jacket, because one of them is the black XR logo on a pink background. She says, "Oh we have extra!" and she calls through the crowded lobby to her husband, who fishes two out of his jacket pocket. One is a green and blue background with the XR logo, and the other is the XR logo on a pink background. She smiles and says that they made them for a woman in her group that only wears orange and pink. I nod and smile, as I love bright crazy colors and sparkles when I'm not wearing all black, which might be another feature of the joy-doom continuum from my mother, and it's always a struggle to stay in the middle, where things are okay or medium, which is Buddhism.

Y. asks if there are more pink buttons, and the woman says, "Oh that was the last one." I offer Y. mine and say, "Look I have two." No, she smiles, thanking me. Neon colors remind me of junior high fashion in the eighties, and then in the nineties there was a kind of shift toward the muted pastel palette of The Limited, which sold Shaker sweaters and mock turtlenecks, so I stayed in that muted range and in flannels but then discovered thrift stores and found wild garments, joyful colors. In college I bought an embroidered woven blousy top from the 1970s and it made me so happy, and since then I either am wearing black and gray or bright pops of color, and I learned that bright color could fish me out of depression, could distract people during the day from my eyes and to my clothes, and usually my spirit would rise to the occasion of acting like a human inside a bright dress, a reminder that there was brightness in the world especially beneath the low gray ceiling of a Midwestern winter sky, including in wartime, and there was always war being waged somewhere far away in our name.

More of us gather, and there's the man in the robe, a Buddhist—is he some kind of monk? He's the one organizing the meditation action, and I reach out to hug him, and there's a slight hippie smell on him that reminds me of Farmhouse, the vegan co-op where I lived for a year in college in Minnesota with a bunch of geology students and a bunch of humanities people angsting about whether they were queer and declaring themselves in love with other people's significant others and breaking up with each other. The geologists might have been queer too but they had so much less angst about it and had the steadiness of geologic formations to ground them. I think rocks, too, are a fine sexual preference. And though it was a vegan co-op, I was raised on sausage and bratwurst and German meats, so I didn't last long as a vegan, though I tried. I was so hungry that after a few months, I went into town and got a pizza with gyro meat and tzatziki sauce on it, and I can still remember the exact ecstatic taste, sitting in a booth with my friend Sol, and it was better than sex. I have had significant pseudo-sexual experiences in Greek diners with friends eating greasy food.

C. is there in the lobby with her husband, and we ask how her shoulder is, she says, "Oh it's completely fine, it was just the weird position we were in with the handcuffs." And then she retells the story about Terry Gross and the burst appendix again and we shake our heads in disbelief.

I pin the two XR buttons on my ribbed white gray and black turtleneck at the place where you put your hand when you say the Pledge of Allegiance, remembering that in grade school we just called it Pledge-a-llegiance, and the pins go in and out of the thin fabric and clip, piercing the thin cotton-poly blend fabric. The shirt was a present from my mother-in-law a few Christmases ago, and I like how it makes me look. Ribbed turtlenecks remind me of the 1970s though I was just a kid then. I have other ribbed turtlenecks, like that black one I bought sometime after college that disintegrated on me over time because I wore it so much. They make me feel slim without being too tight and seem kind of sophisticated in a 1970s way. I think I bought the black one in New York City near Astor Place at some discount store that sold big chunky 1990s shoes, where I bought a black leather pair with a thick heel that made me feel like a rock star until they fell apart.

Sitting on the wooden bench, I take a selfie with the buttons in the courthouse, and it turns out in the photo that I am kind of knowingly smirking, when in real life I don't feel like I ever know anything. A photo of me in vacant doubt looks a little doomy, as my resting thinking face has a bit of a scowl. I debate whether to post it on social media, because I don't suppose I should be open about any part of getting arrested, not because I'm ashamed— and really, what was the point of the action, if not to get attention? Still, given the work firestorm last year, I probably need a break before I start off another one. So I post it as "courthouse selfie" and add an XR hashtag. Anyone who's paying attention could figure it out.

A NATIONAL LAWYERS' GUILD lawyer calls us together, and we stand and gather in a thick circle in the lobby around him. He is old and so incredibly thin he looks like a marionette with a beard and sparse gray hair and gold wire-rim round glasses. He's wearing a red tie and a gray vest, and he good-naturedly talks us through everything that will happen in the courtroom. He tells us our choices about a plea, how entering a guilty plea would send us to sentencing, how a plea of innocent would lead to a trial, and they recommend ACD, which I later learn means "adjournment in contemplation of dismissal."

The French student from our police wagon asks if a trial would be televised, and I think dear effing jesus. The lawyer tells us we're all going to walk into the courtroom together as a group, because this is a political action too. Someone holds open the huge heavy wooden doors, and we walk up the aisle. We file into the rows, in and around the people who are here alone in stress because something in their lives has nudged them to do something they either regret or do not regret, but that either way has caused a lot of complicated trouble for them.

I end up next to the older man who was in my arrest group, and then I let him go by me and scoot over so he can sit next to his wife. Then I'm sitting next to a guy I don't know. The judge goes up and sits in the wooden box and there are people at all the desks doing stuff, shuffling and sorting papers and putting papers in vertical metal slots and clicking things on laptops. Time is different. There are many pauses, like there were in jail, and it's hard to know what they mean. There is a regular slamming sound, almost like the gates of justice clanging, but then I realize it's probably a huge stapler, it just echoes really loudly in here. It's cold so I put on my jacket. There's a metal vertical file near a standing desk to the left of the judge's desk, which is more of a raised box, and I guess that would be a "stand"? The metal vertical file holds a row of manila folders in slots, and a man with glasses pulls the folders one by one and reads things in them to the judge, I guess for each separate case, and the folders are reused and so old and worn that their paper edges are frilled and thickened. They look like they've been saved and reused since the age of Bartelby, the Scrivener.

A folder is taken and opened and a name is called out. A stocky man wearing a black T-shirt comes forward, stepping aside as someone opens the chain across the aisle and then reclasps it behind him. The man needs a Spanish-speaking interpreter. Apparently he bought drugs and thought he would get a different penalty than what is currently being discussed. There are pauses for back-and-forth translation, and he is very soft spoken. His lawyer is young, with a bobbed haircut, and she looks very tired. I wonder how young she is, and I think of my friend Monica, who worked as a public defender after she went to law school at Northeastern in Boston. We met while working at the youth home in Cambridge and then lived together in an apartment in Central Square that had mold on the bathroom ceiling, and the drug dealers on the corner waved hello at us when we walked home at night, and we waved back, and I felt safe. I loved living with her and she helped me grow up without judging me and helped me find a therapist and other help I needed including Al-Anon. After she stopped working at the youth home, she worked at Starbucks and would bring clear garbage bags full of day-old pastries to the youth home and also home for us. I know how hard she worked as a public defender. This lawyer looks hassled and defeated. She explains something to her client through the interpreter, then speaks to the judge, and there's more back and forth with the interpreter and the man, then they decide they need to reschedule. He gets handed a paper by a young smooth-faced bailiff.

THEN A WOMAN IN A BLACK FUZZY COAT and tight black pants gets called up for shoplifting. Each time someone is called up, the bailiff or someone else comes and unhooks the little clasp of the chain that lets the person up near the judge and then re-clasps it behind them like they're going on a rickety ride at the county fair, not like Disneyland where they have thick-posted turnstiles that twirl around and that always somehow seem like they're about to bluntly disembowel you and not even care. The woman asks to be recommended to a theft treatment program, but the bearded lawyer guy who announces the charges can't find information about that program on his phone, and neither can her lawyer. There's a pause and some looking around, some research, and she's deferred to somewhere, given a paper.

I wonder what she stole. I know a lot of people who have shoplifted, me included, my crime being a very nineties fake-silver thick choker chain from Urban Outfitters in my twenties when I was living in Boston, furloughed from a nonprofit, and couldn't buy much and just wanted one nice thing. This woman looks defeated. Something is going on with her, resentment. I get it. I can't summon up the exact feelings I had when I pock-eted the necklace but it did have to do with having no money, the youth home not paying me enough, so that I did not feel at liberty to buy candy or soft drinks from 7-Eleven. Everything was titrated out, the debit card balance hovering close to zero, no health insurance when I started, hourly pay midnight to 8 a.m. I remember the itchiness of being in Cambridge, working at a bookstore, all the rich people at Harvard and visiting Harvard, how once in a while you just want something nice. Taking earrings I found in the lost and found after they'd been there so long we were going to throw them out. Other people I know have stolen because it seemed to them like the store made it too easy; New Yorkers confess to this in a way that I think would shock Midwesterners. Maybe it would not shock Midwesterners, but I think it would.

I PECK OUT AN EMAIL on my phone as we wait in the courtroom, a reply to my friend D. because I had posted something on Twitter about being on state healthcare and WIC when my son was born in response to the Trump administration's latest attempt to slash public benefits, and in the email D. sweetly shares his own story, the dear stories that are buried in academics' past and that are so hard to see but so necessary, because everyone assumes that everyone else has always had money and they are the weird one. If I could, I would carry a scepter of former public aid, a permanent ceramic painted creation, if it would help dispel some misapprehension about who was once poor enough to be desperate.

I reply to an email from a student who was sorry she missed class today because she was sick; a colleague is subbing for me and I feel like I always feel toward the end of the semester like each student had his or her own story and I want all of them to end things well and be okay and get their grades and credit, not waste their expensive tuition by getting sick or dropping out or having a crisis. By the end of the semester, my gradebook in Blackboard is always kind of a mess and never adds up right, so I have to adjust it and refigure it, and the students are stressing, and the ones who have some kind of extra stress like family trauma or mental health stuff or money problems or all of the above are in some cases teetering on the edge, and when they miss classes I email them and start to worry because I don't want them to go under. They get so shy and so filled with shame. Sometimes if we talk a lot, I tell them in a vague way that I have been there. I think they often don't believe me.

The phone up at the front of the courtroom rings, and the judge gets onto a long phone call, stretching out the phone cord as he turns to one side of the wooden stand. My anxiety rises, like maybe he's going to get called away and we'll all have to wait an hour, or get called back another time, get trapped in some Kafkaesque legal whirlpool. That's where my head goes after sitting in a courtroom for a grand total of maybe twenty minutes: Kafka. While people have been in ICE custody for years. But then the judge hangs up the phone, and he calls out an apology to the courtroom for the delay. In the moment after he says "I apologize," a wash of fear comes over me, a wincing, and in my head I cower.

This reaction—because I have time to think about it, sitting here in the courtroom—shocks me. I had expected for an irrational moment that somehow we had irritated him, and that the apology would be followed by a lashing out at us, that making him say "I'm sorry"—did we make him?—will lead to it being so much worse for us. I mull this over, off and on, for the rest of the day. The echo of that flash of terror toward an authority figure thrums and ebbs like a horizon.

My baseline for reactions to other humans is all messed up. In every uncertain situation with a man in charge I am right back to the irrational fear, or maybe it's entirely rational, of the worst moments of power imbalances, the rages I have seen. I assume here that there's a recoil for having a man apologize in public that will lead to punishment. No. Punishment is a one-time thing you grit your teeth through. Payment is what I fear: "You'll pay," the protracted targeting of someone's rage that could last for years, that could be stored up to be doled out, with old crimes heaped out on top of new. Hell, most jobs do the same thing to you, or maybe there are some people who have better boundaries and defenses. I have so many bells and whistles and wind chimes; I am a rattling case of bones and tambourines from old fears. Send a puff of air in my direction and I will confess to you, at this point, that it's better that we die than live forever, because I would keep collecting fear until I was a ball, a knot, nonfunctional.

But the judge doesn't rage at us, doesn't make us pay, doesn't blame us, doesn't yell. He sits down, continues with his work as a judge, and I am shocked. Maybe it's Trump that is making irrational retribution even more of the new normal in my head.

EVENTUALLY THE PROCESSING OF CASES reaches our folders and names, and we are called up in groups, three at a time, and the NLG lawyers or another courtroom person steps back to unhook the chain and snap it back closed behind us. When my name is called with two others, I feel that tiny burst of victory like when my number is called in a deli, but shot through with trepidation. We go up and I am standing next to the lawyer, a different one than in the lobby, graying and taller. I look at the side of his shaved face, and he smiles at the judge and I feel comforted. "ACD," he says after each of our names is read, as a routine. I compose my face to nod wide-eyed, good white girl. The nakedness of standing near a judge is intense, and I don't even look at his face or in the direction of his body, I just look down. How brief your time with the judge is, after all the prep work. How grateful I was, in the moments my divorce was granted in Georgia in that courtroom painted a muted shade of turquoise, that I hadn't been exaggerating, that I had been treated in a manner that a judge in Georgia considered bad, that I wasn't a "crazy bitch."

But in this moment in the courtroom there is no reckoning. The judge calmly and quickly, with no note of scorn or annoyance in his voice, says "ACD" and some other legal language. How different it has been, how different it will be, with the Black Lives Matter protestors whose charges have sometimes been and will be ratcheted up to felonies, as if breaking glass were such a massive crime in the face of centuries of murder. The lawyer gives us each a packet of stapled papers, and we are told to go back to our seats.

I sit down, and now I am next to the robed monk, and he whispers with a goofy smile, "What does your picture look like?" I don't know what he's talking about at first, but he nods down at my packet, so I flip the pages to a picture of me right after I was led into the police station, looking completely hassled and bulky, my hair all stringy and awry (even in an arrest photo I'm harassing myself, not thin or sexy enough after sitting in a police wagon in handcuffs) and we laugh, and in that little-kid sweet moment I trust him completely, this monk whose name I don't even know. He's not a dude all tied up in his holy Buddhism, and I say that as a Buddhist. He's just a guy who happens to meditate and likes to laugh. Versus the sticky cloying "spiritual" texts that a friend sends me occasionally, a chain of insights that are so un-funny kitsch-serious and childish and that often have cartoon animals and reminders to love yourself. I think that might work for some people, but it's too cutesy for me. My spiritual insides look, I think, like an old hardware store in which a can of Cheez Whiz has exploded: just a fucking mess. Anything cute or calm seems to diminish the level of cleanup required but also the hopelessness of the task, and one of my main needs is to laugh at the catastrophe and yet to not hate it, to proceed and to clean the spiritual Cheez Whiz off one hex nut.

I am still giggling with the monk and I feel a stab of guilt because I know we are not supposed to be happy and jokey in this setting; we're white people about to get off scot-free for a group action that was partly built on our privilege of being able to do a dramatic action designed to have favorable media coverage, partly based on our whiteness, so that we would have few if any consequences. But we feel free anyway, as we are, maybe reminded exactly *how* free we are. I do feel set free of something. I have brought something to completion. The last guy to go up goes up alone and he has entered in a short statement that the bearded lawyer reads, and maybe that was the guy on the text chain this morning. Then the smooth-faced lawyer is putting on a red ski jacket over his suit coat so I lean over and say to the people down the pew that I think we can go.

We all get up to go in a mass of parkas and bags with zip-pockets and advanced degrees, and the people who remain sitting in the courtroom look at us as we head toward the door at the back. I make eye contact with a guy sitting in a row to my right, and there's no malice but you can tell there's a question in his eyes about what we all did to be processed as a group, we who look like an army of adjunct professors or a gaggle of graphic designers who have gotten lost on the way to the farmers market.

Outside, back in the lobby, a surge of impatience rises up my throat. People are mulling around slowly, and I am eager to dash away, get to the train, spend the hours sitting, then make it to the Starbucks parking lot by 2 p.m. in Connecticut near the high school to pick up my son. R. is near me and someone says, "Let's do a picture on the courthouse steps!" Apparently someone posted in the text app a picture of the group that had gone through court the previous week. I don't want to wait. I hug R. and say goodbye to a few other people and leave. I detach from the group, barely saying a word to people I've had this intense experience with. When I feel like I'm going to be late for something, I am a pointed arrow, a worried bird.

I text Cliff that I'll be fine with getting Ivan and taking him to the driving test, and Cliff replies with a text of "okay" like a laconic telegraph operator. He is admittedly a twentieth-century man whose main text reference point is books rather than acronyms and emojis. I know this, and yet every time he sends me an "okay" I have a moment when I wonder if maybe he doesn't love me anymore. This is not true, but this style of communication is the opposite of mine, the exclamation points and hearts in every communication, as if . . . as if I loaded extra love into the bubbles of pixels, then some might break through the screen to the wires to the person on the other end. I guess it's that I assume everyone else needs as much reassurance as I do, whereas many people like Cliff don't seem to question daily that they are loved. I mean I know that I am loved, but it is an intellectual act of belief, like believing in geometry. I don't know whether this is the absence of a spiritual faith, or the gap of something else, some substance in me like a thinned protective membrane, and so I have more cracks, and the dust of the world gets in.

I leave, go back out through the lobby, out the doors and through the blue stone entryway and into the street. Now, because I have passed through the process, because it has acknowledged me as a person, I feel freer to be a tourist. I turn and take a picture of part of the inscription atop a curved wall of stone: "Where law ends, there tyranny begins." Right there, in the crack between the two continents of law and tyranny, is where we live, some closer to the edge than others. The air has been warmed by the sun, and light comes down onto the street, warming my face, my head, my back. I'm a normal person again, anonymous.

I walk up the street, and there's a Chinese souvenir store jammed and hung with Buddhas, which I can't resist. I duck in, in a mood of celebration, after all my rushing to be away. I look at the strands of beads on red-and-green cords, a pig statue with a baby's face, and bunches of jade charms. I stop in front of a shelf lined with statues of Guanyin, the Chinese Buddhist deity of compassion, connected to the Tibetan Chenrezig, both forms of Avalokitesvara, he or she of shifting genders who created the world. Guanyin usually holds a tipped vase that is said to contain endless tears of compassion for the universe and its pain. She was the first statue I bought, a tiny, solid, metal commitment, about two inches tall and brass, from a World Market in Columbus, Ohio, after Ivan was born when things were hard and I needed some new anchor, when I first committed to Buddhism after ten years of reading about it. The small statue was not a purchase I took lightly; it felt very significant to take a serious religious step away from Catholicism, from the family in Arkansas where my grandmother went to Latin mass every day. Though she died when I was eight, she's still kind of hovering always in my peripheral vision, along with the nuns, my aunts.

My Aunt Rosy, my favorite, died a few years ago, and when I decided to be a Buddhist at that moment of extended crisis in my life, I worried I would lose her, or that she would feel like I was rejecting her. It turns out that she's done plenty of things to anger the Catholic Church, and I just wanted her to love me, and she continued to do so. I honestly needed something more than a guy bleeding from various wounds who told me to turn the other cheek. I'd tried so hard, started going to Mass again after I got into Al-Anon because they said to find a Higher Power, but I just felt no sense of shelter as I went to Mass wearing jeans with the chain from my maroon chain wallet scraping against the wooden pew. I'll never not be a Catholic, and I love so much about the religion. But faith itself, the concept of faith, the action of faith in Jesus, was not enough instruction. I dug Mary, and she always seemed to reference love, but I needed something fiercer than her downcast eyes as she accepted the broken body of her loved son. Meditation and the dharma protectors wreathed in skulls and fire gave me more of an owner's manual for my brain.

Anyway the Guanyins here in this gift shop are large, about five inches high, happily swirled glass or plastic, white and light green fake jade. They're $30, which some internal censor tells me is too much, and I have a lot of Buddhas in my house, maybe five, which I don't know, is that too many? Attachment to the trappings of Buddhism is spiritual materialism, as Chögyam Trungpa Rinpoche wrote about, a super-helpful concept, and yet I cannot help it, I am forever in love as a Catholic with the tiny plastic statues of saints. I'm also embarrassed at some level to be in a gift shop contemplating buying things after going to court for an environmental protest. I am always, no matter what, a Catholic still confessing my sins.

And then in a felt-lined tray on a table near the door, amid piles and rows of jade statues, necklaces, charms, and beads, I see two glass eggs lying in a little compartment, each about an inch and a half high, swirled in red, yellow, orange, and white. The fact that there are only two increases somehow the sense that I should get one for Ivan, balancing out the ever-present undertow that any purchase at any time is unnecessary (and which I never-theless often override at TJ Maxx.) I pick one up, feeling the cool smooth glass in my palm, the magic of glass, how the roughest substance, sand, becomes the smoothest. The egg is about the size of a robin's egg, with a rough spot at the base where the glass must have been attached to a stem.

I remember seeing glass blowers at a cranberry glass tour somewhere in Virginia, maybe, when we were little and my dad was traveling for work, measuring whether the X-ray equipment at hospitals was leaking. We dropped him off and took the van to the glass factory, where we bought a square little spouted cran-berry-colored jug that I assume we still have somewhere in my mom's house, I think, with ripples along the base. While he was surveying the hospital X-ray equipment with his Geiger coun-ters, my mom would find things for us to do in whatever town we were in. She always found factories for us to tour because she was amazing like that and also maybe because she was raised by a socialist mining family in Germany who did those things, who went to see workers working because work was honorable, and because it was fascinating for kids. I just thought this was normal tourist activity, never really reflected on it until I asked her about it. It reminded me that whenever we went to Germany, my uncle would take us on a drive to go see the mine tipples where my great-grandfather and so many others had worked. So anyway we saw glassblowers swirling and blowing their glowing orange magical goo, the way they worked with gloves and soot and fire and against gravity, bulbous viscosity, the rolling of vases and bowls and the pulling and attaching of rounded accents like fiery taffy. I remember they used a kind of pad, maybe leather, on a long pole, holding it against the twirling blob of gooey glass to shape and round it.

So this egg has a satisfying solidity, and the pattern must have been formed of multiple canes of colored glass and twirled together. I'm surprised I know that name, canes—is that right? I think I learned it in a museum display about Venetian paperweights. The swirls loop and fold into each other, with a red curl at the top that reminds me of the end of an umbilical cord, the fresh twirl on my son's rounded apricot-colored stomach, the miracle of this creature who was grown inside me and who knew me but also did not know me at all, who came from an egg himself.

These eggs were glass, not plastic, so that tipped things in their favor. Plus they were a sign of color from childhood, swirled like the marbles I played with as a kid with my brother and sister. In the 1970s and 1980s we had a collection of marbles in a reddish Folgers coffee can that, we knew, were old fashioned and special; I think my mom had bought them at a flea market. Or they had been bought in dribs and drabs, added to over time. Each marble had its own history and solidity, with interesting splashes of color, red or orange and blue, white, swirls of moss and sea-green and moody sky gray-blue, and some were made of different kinds of clay and glass. They were of a different species than the marbles you could buy in mesh bags at the drug store, which were either all green tinged or all ribboned simply with primary colors in clear glass, and some of them were irregularly shaped, dented or oblong.

These marbles were so special that we named them, though the names were not amazing, like Claude or Randy. They were little-kid names, like Bluey for a blue-green densely swirled large marble, and Mouth for a white marble with a perfect orange-red set of almost-lips and a swash of similar color on top like a toupee. We didn't play marbles, my brother and sister and I, though we were aware that there was a game called Marbles that kids in older, purer times had played, like in the Little Rascals show when they drew a circle outside on the dirt. But how had they done it? Whenever we tried to snap a larger shooter against a smaller marble it hurt our thumbs, plus marbles didn't roll well on shag carpeting.

Instead, we raced them by pushing them down lengths of orange Hot-Wheels racetracks, which you stuck together with these plastic oblong connectors. We got the track in a big card-board box taped up with masking tape at a garage sale. We even had a loop-de-loop. So we'd run two tracks down the stairs, down the off-white carpeting in our split-level house, and we'd run the marbles down, and they'd land at different places on the carpet and the ones that got the farthest past the end of the track were the winners. I remember this being very absorbing because the marbles seemed like perfect beings, with their solid cool weight that nevertheless warmed in your palm, catching and reflecting the living heat of your body. They didn't have eyes, so it was like they were keeping their thoughts to themselves, but they certainly had thoughts and feelings and experiences and memories, I believed.

For a moment standing in the gift shop I wonder if Ivan might like to take an art class, glassblowing, but then that reminds me of pipes and one-hitters and I think okay better not to suggest that. I was a big suggester of activities when he was little and he was a big no-sayer, though he did do art camp a few summers. Thinking about glass-blowing takes me down a tangent of sadness about my ex, though now I think that nobody really thinks pot is a problem, and I didn't think you could have a problem with pot and I had no idea that pot could make someone anxious, mean, and angry. I worry now that it's legal in so many places, we are not yet talking about the ways it can be used badly, like even cough syrup or really anything else can be. Anyway, Ivan is having a whole life of different experiences. I go and pay $5 for the egg at the register, and the woman puts the bag in a tiny Ziploc bag for me, and I tuck the egg into a dark inside pocket of my shoulder bag.

Somehow it's the beautiful glass egg in my bag that makes me think I should write about this day, because it's a beating glowing bright heart of surprise. But then I have to fight with myself, like right, typical of you to choose a day to write about where you seem all activist-y and engaged, and is this all a smokescreen for the days in which you're completely passive and complicit or the most interesting thing you do is laundry and going to TJ Maxx? And then is this inner bully yet another smokescreen to show how aware I am, to deflect feared external criticism? Russian nested dolls. What is my head really like when I'm not afraid of being judged? I'm okay. Doing my best is what's needed, and the other half is nudging myself a little bit outside of my comfort zone, and that's why my friend Barbara says today and this week have been so hard for me, and she's right. Could I just stop judging myself? So the egg made me happy, and it, like blown glass, seems to have a consciousness to it, and a combination of cool and warmth, that causes the day to kind of orbit around it.

I find the Canal Street subway station and take the 6 train up to Grand Central with no problem, enjoying the look of the orange seats on the subway train: they are grouped in pairs with different shades, sort of a light orange, then medium, then darker, and I wonder if it would be possible to sit people down on those seats in shirts that exactly match those shades. This might be funny to do, just like you could do it in a Denny's restaurant anywhere in America, but if you do it in New York you're suddenly an icon channeling the voice of your generation. I know that's not true but Cliff and I laugh at the huge numbers of novels set in Brooklyn, as if anyone outside of Brooklyn cares about Brooklyn more than any other place. It doesn't harm me in any way that New York is very solipsistic about itself, and sure it's fine to have hometown pride, but what about Indianapolis. And I'm thinking about color because I'm not as anxious anymore, and color is my home in the world. (I read some quote in college decades ago about how anyone who chooses color over form is a coward, so I've always felt guilty about that, even though I have no idea if this was the right quote or where it came from, and now it's just a piece of educational shrapnel.) I'm so relaxed that one of my jobs today is done, and there's a kind of sleepiness of the adrenaline ebb mixed with an edginess to be vigilant for all the next right steps.

The subway station near Grand Central seems almost familiar to me now, which again fills me with a kind of pride at learning a system, or expanding my notion of home to include this busy place. I cross the gray-green tile floor with an inlaid mosaic of a compass, and for a second my brain doesn't know where it's supposed to go, but then I let my body choose a direction and it ends up being the right way to Metro North, up a passageway, and then into a door to Grand Central. There's a cluster of three people near a kiosk where train times are listed, a quick flash of conversation about a woman in some kind of a dilemma and they don't know what to do.

I cross the main hall, looking for the track number for the train to New Haven, amid an afternoonish crowd of people moving more sluggishly than commuters, people thinking about snacks or wasting time. I take stairs down to the dining area, hunting for the bathroom, and I end up on a tiled mezzanine with a ramp that heads down past an oyster bar I hadn't seen before. I loop around the edge of the dining kiosks, some closed, most with no lines. The women's bathrooms in Grand Central are my home base in Manhattan, as they are probably everyone's who doesn't live here, because it's really hard to find a place to pee in the city. So when I'm in line near the Shake Shack heading for the door on the right to the ladies room, I feel protected. I take a right turn into that warren of stalls, a place where, day and night, all kinds of nervous transitions are happening: sickness, travel, changing to go out, standing in one shoe and trying to pull on pantyhose for a job interview when you know you won't get the job, looking at your eyes in the mirror and trying to look different than how you are. The doors are solid and slam emphatically when someone leaves, and the bathroom traffic always moves at a good respectable clip, which I like, as a woman who prides herself on peeing so much faster than most of her sisters. I don't

SUPREMELY TINY ACTS · 129

know why it takes women so long to pee but I imagine it's partly tampons, partly complicated outfits, and part of it is just taking one goddamn second to breathe before heading out into the goddamn exhausting world. I can't remember but I think I put my shoulder bag on the floor as I pee, which I know is not good, because for damn sure there's e. coli on the floor and god knows what else, and I do not disinfect the bottoms of my shoulder bags, though I guess I should. But I would also feel bad if I put my huge shoulder bag on one of the old-looking metal hooks on the back of the door and broke it off with the weight of the bag.

I leave and wash my hands in the steel oval shallow sink, which is sort of low even for me, below hip level and small. Beneath each soap dispenser between the sinks and mirrors is a big absorbent yellow towel. It looks really dense, like felt, and designed by science to be super-absorbent, and this somehow makes me happy, that this isn't a normal rag that will quickly get soaked and soppy and mildewy and sit in a puddle of its own overwhelm. These are yellow experts that are ready for their mission.

For some reason this reminds me of working at Pizza Hut— was it Pizza Hut, or another of my food service jobs? It was Pizza Hut, and there were white towels we used to wipe down the food surfaces that were called "Chix." This was probably their brand name, and they had kind of a nubbed pattern with a threading maybe of blue, and in the restaurant the towels that we were currently using lived in a white plastic bucket of bleach water. "Get me another Chix" was what you would say instead of "Get me a towel," for no reason I could understand. Anyway, weird that the word carried a reminder of "baby chicks" or "Hey, Chick, what's shaking?" but was neither.

On the wall between two stalls in the bathroom is a sign that says "Don't bathe in here." And god bless any soul who has needed to. Like, that should be part of the sign. God bless you. Unless you've just decided to be dirty because you're following Phish, not that I am going to blame you, but that's not the same as not choosing and ending up in that situation. Though I guess this simple binary frays into meaningless eventually, like those Chix towels, which really did get eaten up pretty quickly by their lives in bleach water.

I LOOK AT MY FITBIT and decide I have enough time to eat, since I won't be able to until much later. I leave the bathroom and walk all the way around the edge of the dining area, past Indian, sushi, and burger places and a few nice bakeries, circling what might be a coffee or bar and sandwich place in the middle, and I get sad that I can't find the tacos. For some reason, the tacos at one corner place in Grand Central are another part of my routine. They are very good. So then I find the taco place, and there are two girls standing near the entrance to the line. Maybe they are just waiting for someone and kind of gazing at the selection on the dry-erase board behind the food window? I stand politely behind them, waiting for that weird accrual of presence, like gravity or rainwater, that seems to happen in someone's peripheral vision. Usually even if a person is busy doing or thinking something else, it takes only a few seconds for their head to pull back and to look at you and "Oh sorry, go ahead!" But in this case that doesn't happen, so I ask, "Are you waiting to order?" and they say no—all I remember is that one girl was blonde and one girl's hair was maybe auburn, and they were in their twenties—and then oddly they didn't move. I pause, then gesture with my torso and shoulders as if to step around them. In normal human interaction this would be when they would pull back, sensing they were blocking the line to the register. It's odd. This was a place of travelers. I chalk it up to differences in social cues, they were from somewhere, they are maybe tired and baffled by the idea of their taco options.

I normally get two chicken tacos but I decide to celebrate by ordering two pescado and one pollo. My accent is terrible. It is the Starbucks dilemma. No matter how I order, in whatever language, I feel like an asshole, merely because of the fact that there are two language options. I first had real tacos, like tacos that didn't come from a yellow El Paso cardboard box in the grocery store or from Taco Bell, when my socialist fiancé (first of four fiancés, two of whom were socialists) took me to an island in Mexico called Isla Mujeres in the mid 1990s that was astoundingly beautiful. I'm so glad I went, even though I think we had either just broken up or were just about to break up and there was a hurricane and all the windows were boarded up and pickup trucks with speakers drove around in the howling rain droning instructions to stay inside as we huddled in a very low-budget but safe concrete hotel room. We had tequila and sun and lime, I ate tacos with fish and the tortillas tasted almost soapy and fresh like if you could eat a freshly laundered bedsheet, but in a good way. We rode a motorbike and saw baby turtles. I was always breaking up with B., we had a lot of breakups because he was thirteen years older than me, which I don't think normally matters, but I was a very young and naïve twenty-three, young enough to think that an anarchist dating a socialist would produce some weird ideal fusion of radical theory/praxis that would heal the tensions between the red and the black (the colors are red for socialists and black for anarchists). My theory now seems kind of bizarre, bordering on hope toxicity. That was how I ended up selling the Socialist Worker newspaper in Harvard Square, trying to raise my hand to make "interventions" in meetings, which is what that brand of socialists called it when they made points or arguments. I thought maybe I could get these hard-bitten Marxists to see anarchism as something more organic to the youth culture of post-Cold-War America and less as a petit bourgeois aberration. (Yeah this was how I spent my twenties, and I gather that other people instead worked at publishing houses and watched television shows that I missed and learned how to tend their eyebrows and started grad school.)

Near the register of the taco place in Grand Central there is a little cooler with ice and glass bottles of orange and pink drinks, and the color of the drinks makes me almost want to buy one, even though I know it is probably sugar water, but I don't buy one. I pay and step to the right, waiting for order 82, and then I am strangely embarrassed that mine is ready ahead of the man who ordered before me. A tiny sadness and a tiny victory. I take the plastic rectangular take-out bin that always makes me sad because it's #5 plastic with a black base and clear top, and I believe this number is harder to recycle than others, but really, is anything being recycled in the aftermath of whatever happened in China, probably Trump's trade war, that made it no longer profitable for China to do our recycling. It's probably a hazardous process, which means we should do it ourselves but where, what is happening to all the plastic, and should I be that person that says to the woman behind the counter, "Oh can you just put it in a little paper boat? I don't need it hermetically sealed, I am not going on a long journey, I'm going to go right around the corner and devour these things in a second." That's what I should have done. But instead of being ethical I prefer to not interrupt anyone's normal routine, I prefer to just glide along and offer zero speedbumps, not to be a trouble, be a horrid good girl.

Sitting there eating a fish taco with amazing spicy light-orange sauce that runs down along my pinkie finger, onto the outside flesh of my hand and a bit down my wrist, I am proud that I can now go into New York and back without it exhausting me. When I first moved here, a few years after getting diagnosed with rheumatoid arthritis, almost any travel-type mobilization of any sort would land me in bed for the next day. Things are much better now, the meds have truly helped, my stress has decreased, it's less humid up in Connecticut, and I'm getting less afraid to push myself a little, but not too much, like finding that sweet spot in the clutch on a manual car.

The laminated square tabletop is decorated with a scatter of ticket stubs, old subway tokens, and schedules from the commuter rail, including the schedule for a bunch of trains that branch off the two main lines into Connecticut, and I wonder if those offshoot lines still run. The fish is very spicy, impossibly good, with pale green grated cabbage as a garnish, and it's perfect, a squiggle that's hard, cool, and almost tasteless, and it works because it's just a little line to bring out the opposites around it. There's something so beautiful about a tiny inch-long squiggle of cabbage, because cabbage is the bowling ball of vegetables. To hack it apart is an athletic act, first from the stalk, then the outside leaves, then cutting it into two hemispheres, then grating or slicing with a huge knife, and cutting at such an angle so as to produce not rough trapezoids but instead delicate cross-sections of a leaf layer when that leaf is rippled enough to produce interesting variation. To start with something so big and produce just a tiny fleck speaks to a kind of sculptural grandness. And I'm so used to eating it as sauerkraut that I forget it's completely edible as a raw thing.

I take a book out of my bag that I brought with me in addition to all the grading and writing, which is called *Messy: The Power of Disorder to Transform Our Lives.* I bought it because, well, I'm a messy person and I wanted to be enabled and to be told that my slovenliness is a sign of brilliance or that it's at least functional. The book has a nice cover, illustrated with a bunch of colored Post-its and rubber bands in bright colors on a white background, and it has science and a nice narrative style, though it isn't exactly what I was expecting. Instead of enabling me, it's a series of examples of how chaos or breaks or introduction of new processes lead to discoveries. I open the book on the table and feel like maybe I could make myself believe I am on vacation: look, a book and tacos in a train station! But I'm too tired to focus and also kind of holding myself back from falling into the book, preoccupied. I instead just kind of look at the texture of the paper, which is cream-colored and somewhat rougher than I'd expect for a hardback book. I look at the train time app on my phone and I'm thrilled I have time, that I don't have to rush.

I finish my tacos and consider the rectangular black plastic shallow container. Should I seal it, slip the container in my bag, take it home, and put it in the dishwasher, then either shove it in the messy cabinet in our kitchen filled with twenty similar containers in a ridiculous disarray? It's a kind of prayer I do, the reflexive wondering of how to dispose of the remains. I don't want taco juice to leak out into my bag and get all over my papers. So I put it in the trash and feel a thrill of doomy badness, like I'm just being a regular person and that's satisfying because my relationship with that piece of plastic is *over.* It reminds me of Jason, the first anarchist I met in college, who told us that he didn't believe in recycling because we weren't going to change the world that way, and all of us good girls on the environmental committee were shocked, looking at him goggle-eyed, like *How can you not recycle?* But he was right, but then again, it was easy for him to take that dramatic stance and much harder for us in the late eighties to have the real conversations with the university that led them to put a barrel in the mailroom and get a contract to ship the paper to someplace that would buy it for making cardboard. There is always the glamorous radical stance and then there is whoever is left making the fucking pot of lentils (as I say to myself, as a person who has had to make the lentils). Eventually I came to see the making of the lentils as the radical act, and equally as radical was not drawing a binary between those plain lentils and the "revolution" somewhere in the future. Obsessions with the future, including what we have to put up with in the present to get there, have not served me well.

I double check the screens to see the listing for the 11:34 on track 19. I get up and go down the hallway to the train, luckily not all the way up on the top level but instead down here in the close steam- and ash-smelling tunnel. The train is on the left-hand track, and I'm early, so I stand on the concrete platform at an odd distance from others who are also waiting, each either near a door that they have selected as being the right distance from one end of the train or the other. I go down a few cars and stand with that weird stab of fear like, what if we all think this is the right train but then they change it and don't tell us? Some people are leaning against the dirty pillars, and there's no phone reception here in the tunnel beneath the station so I can't really look at my phone, though I can play the dot game if I want. I look at the red dots of light on the display near the closed door, which spell out "New Haven" and I reach in my bag and touch my book, think I could read, but then I think I could be one of those people who uses a pause to meditate.

Looking inside my brain during the day—instead of when I'm prepared, on a meditation cushion with a lit candle—is a little like catching my brain naked in a kitchen making an omelet with its hair a mess. It looks at me like, "What the fuck, I'm working, why are you—aren't you supposed to be busy—" and then puts down the omelet pan and says *okay fine* and sits on the linoleum and goes into itself, as you do when you meditate: the mirrors upon mirrors upon the pulse and the consciousness of one's own spinal column, vertebrae, really inside one's body at this present moment, pinkish and mauvish organs actually functioning, things I'm resisting, what am I fighting with, I'm fighting with the limitations of my own body, I'm afraid of my own tiredness, I'm worried I'm not a good mom, okay, let it just. . . simmer . . . and then something releases . . . for a micro-second . . . and the train doors open.

I go in and turn right down the aisle, looking for a seat that faces forward. I remember as a child throwing up on a bus to Switzerland, and then getting my whole family kicked off the bus. We had to wait for hours for my uncle to come pick us up. We spent lots of time in one small town in Germany where my mom was born, but we didn't really travel in Europe ever. So that bus trip was my mother's grand attempt to travel away from the small industrial town of her birth, the first time we were casting outward to see the sights alone, and then I ruined it by barfing on my lap just a few hours later. There were fumes in the bus, in my defense, and somehow the seats were high up, or the bus was high with a luggage area beneath, which meant that every turn sort of made us rock to and fro, and I was not even sitting next to anyone from my family, though I was near the window, and the barfing came despite knowing that I always got car sick and had thrown up in cars before but for some reason we didn't travel with Dramamine. Or maybe I threw up irregularly enough that it wasn't seen as a predictable issue.

Anyway, I must have been younger than seven, and I remember being yelled at by the bus driver and being covered with puke and then sitting on a bench outside a corner store with my family, where I'm sure I was crying and apologizing, and we waited hours until my uncle picked us up, and then I guess we all sat in the closed car smelling my vomit for hours on the ride back home. This is the kind of thing that happened regularly in the 1970s, in the sense that shit just happened, and then when you look back at your memories you think, how could that just have happened? Did it even happen? And today that kind of thing would probably be filmed on twenty smartphones and would bring down a bus company via a scathing social media campaign.

A woman ahead of me in the train aisle struggles with two suitcases, and whenever I see someone with suitcases getting to MetroNorth I know they've had a long way to go, it's not easy at all to get to the airport to the bus to the subway to the train. It's exhausting. She wrestles with putting a suitcase that is too large into the overhead rack, and I slip by her to get out of her way and get a perfect seat that feels enclosed and safe and no one sits next to me. I'm so drowsy. I half-sleep as the train pulls out of the station, and I look at my phone, and before I know it we are in Connecticut, and I am thinking about how proud I am of myself that these towns roll by without provoking undue anxiety. Before I know it we are passing Darien. Look at me! It's like I live here! I do live here!

What I mean is that at some point in the past, the mere names of fancy towns like Darien and Greenwich would bring on deep impostor syndrome or ennui or just a deep sadness about wealth disparities and all the memories of not fitting in in places where multiple social classes were gathered all at once, difficulties that have happened at such crazy extremes here on the East Coast in a way that didn't seem as extreme in the Midwest.

I check my phone and there are texts from my wonderful friends Barbara and Hilts asking me how I'm doing, and I say good but exhausted. There are lots of heart emojis in the texts, and I curl up with my knees on the seat in front of me. I can't really even muster a decent response, I'm feeling dead inside, probably from the adrenaline crash that feels like cement in my veins, like being drunk on mimeograph toner. Barbara and Hilts are concerned about me today, maybe because I started crying when we met at writing group on Saturday at Barbara's beautiful little house with a view of the Long Island Sound from Milford at the top of a hill and the needlepoint over the sink that says "I take my coffee very seriously." She had set the table so beautifully with colorful cups and coffee and I don't remember what we ate, but it included soup and it was perfect.

When it was my turn in Barbara's kitchen to talk about what I'd written, very rough pages in a massive book with tons of research, I started to choke up and said I didn't want to talk about them, I needed to vent for a second about how overwhelmed I was. I was in an endless-seeming waiting loop about a big writing project; I had been writing a summary document, a book proposal about that writing project, and then I was asked to write a summary document of the summary document, and I'm not good at summaries. These summary documents were going to a very important publishing company. And I wanted it to go well and signs looked good, but the thing is that I kind of exist in a shadow of clenched muscles and impending doom as it is. Which I know is inappropriate and shows a lack of perspective because my life is great. These are great amazing problems to have, but telling myself I'm a piece of shit for feeling sad is counterproductive on top of everything, and yet that is my go-to.

And that day at Barbara's a week before court, I was overwhelmed looking ahead at the week because that night my son had invited some friends over, was turning sixteen, and I had to pick up an ice cream cake, and then I had to wrap presents, mostly banners and pennants for the New Orleans Saints that he wanted to put up in the basement, and I wanted him to have a good birthday, but was I ever up to providing a good birthday? He was an only child and really wanted siblings, but I had not been in a position to have a second child because of the nightmare exploding first marriage. We had to get out, I had to support us and get out with my wits about me and still work, and I've felt guilty and sad about that forever. And then, too—did I get enough presents or the right presents to make him feel loved? Did he feel loved? Of course he did, but I loved him so much that I went straight to inadequacy.

But he's a good steady son, and every time I look at him or interact with him I think, wow, that had to come from somewhere, all my effort to love him must have come through, even though part of his childhood was completely bonkers. And I was also overwhelmed on Saturday at Barbara's because of the impending court thing, and that scared me at some subconscious level, and then I had to cancel class and it was the end of the semester and my students were all in various levels of tension and need, and I was supervising a grad student project, and then on Wednesday I was giving the webinar about pain and metaphor, and who do I think I am, as always, to think I have anything meaningful to say.

I will not here go so far as to make myself feel bad for doubting myself, as I think there are very specific reasons I view myself askance and wonder every day whether I'll be able to pull off my schedule. I don't think self-doubt is a moral failing, I don't think I can feel better by trying harder, it's a conditioned response. As always I thank god for Al-Anon, which taught me coping skills, and remember that there is such a thing as a higher power even if I steer widely between a Catholic God and the Buddha, who isn't really a HP in the traditional sense but whatever. Parts of my life have been overwhelming and then, sadly, that overwhelm itself has become familiar enough that I steered toward that feeling itself as home. At past times in my life, I have been unable to get out of that loop, though I'm doing so much better these days. The important thing, I said as I was crying at Barbara's kitchen table, is that I've been holding myself hovering above and away from meditation, from any kind of hope or release or rest, because I have this idea that if I stop my feelings, if I don't hope, if I kind of mourn the hurt in advance, it will hurt less when I'm disappointed. I am fully aware that this is irrational. But I'm not shallow enough to paper it over with #blessed and thinking positive inspiration-porn. I just flat-out reject that part of America and I think I'd physically fight it if I could. I imagine fighting someone in a purple costume of Barney the Dinosaur, a kid's program I never liked because that dinosaur is somehow super creepy with tiny eyes and teeth like a gameshow host.

A blessing in my life is that I choose wise and wonderful friends with sick senses of humor. Plus even though I'm scared most of the time, stunned that everyone is buying the long con of this smart 12-year-old in wrinkly skin, one thing I do know how to do is to show up. Oh, I know more than one thing: I know both to keep doing the next right thing and to push myself to do what I'm scared of. I know how much good comes from pure tenacity, and also that the antidote to being scared or over-whelmed is to focus on my to-do lists and taking the next right step. Just doing that, the technology of to-do and next-right-thing, has given me everything I need. But then also the next level: with my fear and my fierceness, the idea of the gentle middle, of being kind and reasonable toward myself, often gets lost. I have built in quite a few to-do's about self-care but then these to-do's also roar like little dragons. I am deeply separated from an innate sense of balance. Maybe it's class and region too—I feel less daunted in the Midwest, less aware of how I'm being evaluated. There I am perceived as more confident, less of a golly-gee person who smiles too much.

Sometimes I wonder if I'm daunted because I'm so nonsequential, so scattered, that seeming organized and linear takes a ton of effort and forcing. I'm a slob, always have been, need to see things laid out visually. Tangents are my strength. My epic to-do lists are all a way to channel my tornado. A tornado both spins and has forward motion. The periods of humor, ridiculousness, and play are a necessary release from the linear dauntedness. I do get a lot of things done and organized, but putting them on the calendar is my absolute least favorite part of it, almost physically painful. It's because each box is so separate and so lonely and they're all the same. I have even tried designing calendars that weren't grids, but really, who has time to design a whole calendar.

The other day in class I told my students, who because of something we read were mourning the ends of their childhoods, that they could keep being young in the most important ways, that they could hold onto the kids inside them. And maybe that's the price I pay for having a direct connection to that scared kid: she's often overwhelmed. I am working on the confidence, but what if having rock-solid confidence means you're dead inside and have lost your capacity for awe, whereas I'm in awe every day? If that's the price, I'm fine with staying the way I am.

I open the *Messy* book and balance it on my knees in the train seat, but I can't focus because I'm so tired. I open my phone and play a truly terrible game where you have to line up gems in a row to make them disappear. It is monotonous, and then I have the concrete satisfaction of winning a free hour of play in the game for the train ride. These are the kinds of things I had to allow myself after Trump was elected. Before I got sick in 2010, my time was very tightly scheduled and I answered a lot of email at night, and then I got sick and had to give myself more and more time to rest, and then with Trump I consciously blocked out still more hours of no-thinking in the evenings. My default was to always try to do useful things, working under the fantasy that getting more done would lead to a break sometime in the future, but that really never happens.

After the election and the crying and the few days where it was hard to get out of bed and more crying, I began to see that

I needed the same kind of strategies I'd always used to manage depression to also manage survival under Trump. And I had to amp it up a bit. So, yes, a higher dose of meds. But at night, I'd read news, and after a certain hour of the evening there was no benefit to mulling over the latest doings of Steve Bannon and Neo-Nazis. More than ever before, maybe for the first time in my life, I began to really understand the biological benefit of stopping my brain cold. The dumber the game the better. I wanted no stress. I wanted Two Dots, Three Gems, whatever. The challenge is extremely low, the stakes are low, the gains are monotonous, the game will never be completed. Actually I think at one point there was a way to win Two Dots, and the thought of that made me angry. I would often do that thing that they tell you is so morally reprehensible somehow, watching something I half cared about on Netflix AND playing a stupid game on my phone at the same time. The reason was because I often feel too emotionally overwhelmed by a story on the screen if it turns violent or dark, or I am bored with it, so playing a game at the same time allows me to exist in a thin hovering space between two digital media that is most like peace or being frozen.

On the train I eat the protein collagen bar, the same flavor as the one I ate in jail and superstitiously bought again for today. This one is also chunky and chalky. I fill in part of a New York Times Crossword on my phone. I also decided at some point in 2017 to pay $40 a year for unlimited access to the archives on the app, so that there is always another crossword puzzle. I find them calming of a level up from the dot games because the substance is words, knowledge, description, and the interface is so orderly and calm. The questions are mostly unpredictable, but it's funny how a certain puzzle author will get into a rut and lean on a certain word to fill in a difficult set: Eon, Era, Ages. Long stretches of time. I cheat. As in, there's a "check" function you can choose so that you immediately can know whether you've filled in the right letter. I play with that on, mostly, because my goal is to keep a steady momentum of engagement, a steady distraction. The crossword puzzles give me nouns and verbs to be grateful for.

The words in the puzzle for this day, November 19, 2019, make a poem that in retrospect sings a song of COVID-19 to me: AGAIN, ELASTIC, WEAVERS, CARDIAC, BRINK, SAD FACE, DON'T ASK, BLEEDER, AIR TUBE, RNA, BRAVURA, RAN AMOK, along with a trio of American figures powerless to offer salvation: ABE LINCOLN, WILLY WONKA, SCROOGE MCDUCK. And oddly, AWE. But of course at the time, I didn't interpret that as anything personal. I was probably just happy to encounter the flash of Gene Wilder's face in the answers, his wistful inscrutable sad smile, in my mind's mirror. And it would later turn out that the first case of COVID-19 emerged in China two mere days before today, on November 17, 2019.

At 12:47 p.m. I receive a text from my pharmacy CVS to renew my Otrexup, which is the brand name for my injection. It's a very slight tweak the drug company made to the formula for the generic, methotrexate, and it happens to work better for many people including me via injection because the pills are hard on the stomach. The injections are hard on my insurance company, I think thousands of dollars a month, because the slight change allows them to make it a brand name and charge a thousand dollars a month instead of $30. And so there's some residual guilt I have, combined with the subconscious knowledge that it's poison, that makes me always delay in refilling my prescription, so that if I were to add the shots up, I'm sure I'm months behind.

I ride the train the whole way home and don't even look at the draft of the article I agreed to do, or the notes for my talk. We pull into the Stratford station, where there are silver metal walkways that stretch out from the platform to the train doors, over a track that for some reason isn't used anymore. I walk along the walkway, down the concrete stairs, underneath the railroad overpass across from the Polish deli and the Vietnamese place, then walk up the ramp to the parking lot, where I feel a little bit more like a real person because I got a real parking space instead of having to cram my car on a side street several blocks away and fear a ticket or being towed.

I drive home, the automatic right turn out of the train station, past my neurologist's office and the church where I have spoken at the open Al-Anon/AA meetings, past the firehouse, past the high school and the gas station on the corner. It's starting to spit rain, and I think as I turn at the post office that maybe I have time for a nap, but I don't. I pull up to our yellow house, open the door, and put my bag down, and the dog is ecstatic with her whacking wagging tail and the spots on her paws and nose, her black soft ears and wild eyes so sure, SO SURE, I'm going to take her out for a nice long walk because it's that time, but I have to say to her *I'm sorry girl, it's not, I can't take you.* I can't even look into her sad hopeful Gene Wilder eyes because I have to pull some papers out of my bag and gather up other paper.

I dodge her as she pummels me with her face and I pull a packet of peanut butter cups out of my bag and rip it open, aiming just to get sugar into my system, and I go to the sink and fill up my water bottle. I take the folder of grading out of my bag. Then I go over to the dining room table. In a basket, for some reason, there's a fake stuffed stork-like egret bird that stands amid papers and knickknacks. We have more stuffed creatures in our house than an average home, including one fish, this weird battered egret, a stuffed squirrel my husband bought at a garage sale, and a papier mâché puffin we had to put high up on a shelf because the cats want to murder it. Anyway, amid the fake stork's feet are a few travel pill cases, some old cannabidiol tincture bottles, some screws and nuts we don't know the origin of, some handouts from physical therapists, and a white envelope I have carefully loaded with all of the ID that proves that my boy exists. It's so odd: it's lighter than a magazine, this packet of all his documentation.

I go over to the chaise part of the couch that sits near the window so Hazel the dog can look out and bark at everything, and she's sitting there despondent, and so I mush at her forehead and she puts her face between her paws like she can't believe I've made such a mistake in rushing off somewhere that does not involve snuggling with her. I kiss her forehead, which always smells like the wind.

I get back in the van, take the turn into the shopping plaza via our daily shortcut, and at 1:49 I text Ivan that I'm in the Starbucks lot opposite his high school. Teenagers with hoodies on and hoodies off mill across the chaotic five-way intersection, loping, laughing. I scan the crowd for him, and all the thin shoulders of the boys remind me of him. I look down. My phone battery is at 17% and I plug it in. Then he's there, near the passenger door, and we glance at each other as he ducks in and smiles.

This is an odd thing that there should be a name for, a kind of internal inflation that unfolds as soon as he's around that deflates when he's away: an invisible mothering organ, much more associated with the heart and brain than the uterus. I become a hypothetical better self. It is almost as though I understand at a cellular level, as I always have, that I have to reassure another person, that in some way I am the membrane between the world and this person, and so I become a steadier and clearer version of myself. It's related to my teaching persona but different, much deeper. The mothering unfolds like drawing water from a communal well, and it echoes down into the center of the earth. The unnamed energy always arrives, but at the same time, that mothering force is always slightly less than one needs, and one always has to fill in the gap. A mother is not a god, but mothering is akin to being a prayer. It is the simultaneous action of translation and protection.

Mothering has, in my limited experience of one child, involved much daring and vulnerability. With a teenager, mothering involves more pauses. One suggests sidelong, trying not to impose, but always to direct the vision, to shape without constraining. Sometimes I think that a third of mothering is about pointing out how pretty the sky looks right now, with the light underneath. That, at least, I have done well.

Rain is splotching on the windshield in round drops, and now traffic and a destination and an appointment and ID are all involved. This is real shit: I have to get a person to a place. I am scanning the roadsides, as I always am with my son in the car, always more careful than when I drive alone, the idea of this most precious cargo always humming in the back of my mind. Plus he's been watching my driving because he's learning to drive, so if I screw up or glance at my phone I look like a huge hypocrite. We take the road named Nichols north toward the Merritt Parkway, a road we take frequently, although I have some kind of mental block against its name. "N" comes into my head and nothing else. Why? When I actually call it "That road I can't remember," my son and husband both know the road I mean. The road is long and busy and goes very important places like Target and the highway. Clearly "Nichols" just doesn't do it for me—it's hardly even a word, the equivalent of five cents. The road needs another syllable, some more vowels. German leads me to want something with more heft, maybe? My one aunt and uncle lived on Leverkusener Strasse, and the others lived on Droste-Hülshoff Strasse, which I think are nice substantial-sounding street names.

On the way to the Hamden DMV I take a slightly longer route because I know Ivan hates to be early, but I have to be early. He hates it when we have to wait places because I've made him do a lot of that, but at least he's used to it. We are going to Hamden, which is a suburb of New Haven. Way before I ever thought I would be living in Connecticut, I once taught an older MFA student who was obsessed with canoeing, was very WASPy and stern and one of his parents died when he was young. Because I didn't have much experience with New England outside of New York and the anarchist institute, I always took New England to be an extension of England, or America in the time of Nathaniel Hawthorne. So I always associated Hamden with the English countryside, where I've also never been. Anyway, this canoeing man with white hair just resisted, as students do sometimes. They sign up because they want to be pushed into writing and cracking open their life stories, and then when you, as the teacher, ask them the questions that emerge from the text they have written, they sometimes squint at you and tell you they don't want to write about that. So then what do you do? You have to say, okay, well, you can have a slightly less engaging and introspective story if you want? It's impossible to make someone write something they don't want to write. I just write diagrams of possibilities on a dry-erase board, like a football coach if the game were the length of your entire life and involved no ball and no scores.

Rain thwacks the windshield. I turn on the wipers as we drive uphill toward Route 15, past the road that leads to Target. Ivan asks me at what speed you can start hydroplaning—he's quizzing me from the driver's ed book—and I guess it's 20 miles per hour but the correct answer is 35. I remember an approach to an intersection, a heart-stopping hydroplane alone when I was his age, the swing and yaw of the car's back end toward the traffic light hanging dimly above, a sleeting night in Illinois, the feeling almost of flying, the terrible slip away from traction.

On the Merritt Parkway I tell Ivan about being in the Bridgeport DMV for eight hours when Cliff and I first moved to Connecticut in the summer of 2011 while he was still staying at his dad's in Ohio. There was some software conversion or budget issue that made the DMV open less often, so it was supercrowded and everything took a long time, and we didn't know that the Bridgeport office was the most crowded always, and we needed in-state licenses to get either utilities or a checking account to get established as residents. People were ordering pizzas to be delivered to the DMV, and the air conditioning wasn't working great. We paced and sat in the hard plastic seats, and then it went from infuriating to hilarious. My picture on the new Connecticut license looked like mayhem, with turquoise dangly earrings, my hair kind of flying everywhere, a semi-delirious smile.

OFF THE MERRITT, THE WAY to the Hamden DMV is circu-
itous and through a marsh-like area past some apartments, very
New Englandy and dark. We find the brown brick building and
I park, and I'm trying to describe how you're supposed to turn
the steering wheel against the direction of a spin when you're
slipping on the ice, even though that's counterintuitive in the
moment. In a flash I realize I've driven in all kinds of weather
that's not anything Ivan has really seen: blizzards in Minnesota
and Illinois, careening off roads into ditches, getting stuck in
snowdrifts.

"It's easier here," I tell him. "In Illinois there was all the snow
and big weather and ice." He looks at me with respect for the
things I know how to do. That happens a lot when you're first
parenting, and then not at all for a while, and so when it happens
with a teenager you savor it.

I have other stories I choose not to tell him right now, like
the time I was driving with my sister in the rain right after she
got her license, and we went to Chicago and I was telling her to
slow down on the curve at the south part of Lake Shore Drive,
and we hydroplaned and the car swung 180 degrees around back-
wards on a northbound curve in Lake Shore Drive so that the
car hit the concrete embankment and careened along it, burning
a small hole in the side of the car. Later we lied to our mom to
explain the hole in the car, but at the time we just made a U-turn
and headed northbound again. How we weren't killed, how we
didn't kill other people, I have no idea. She was Ivan's age and I
was twenty.

We go inside the building and talk to a woman at a podium
and show her the printout for our appointment for his permit
test. We wait and are called up to the gray counter. I am holding

a manila envelope with all of the documents I think we need, but I am never confident about identification. I have collected all the vulnerable tiny bits of paper to prove my son exists, that we exist, and I am sort of amazed that I've managed to file everything correctly. I feel a specific kind of anxiety every time I have to hand over a piece of ID. It doesn't make sense because I'm safe—I have all the right ID, the privilege of a US passport—but it always feels like they're going to find me out as having impersonated myself this whole time. It's like the fear of standing at customs, looking at a person behind a desk when I'm trying to enter a country, always feeling like I'm faking being real, always feeling as a shadow memory the horror of the Holocaust and what my people did to other people, using forms and identification and birthplaces and nationalities. The Nazis searched my grandfather's house after they found his name on a list. He was a leader of the Social Democratic party in their town as his father had been. He had hidden the membership lists and the Marxist and socialist books in the attic beneath the eaves, but someone had narced on him, a comrade. He managed to stay safe and alive, but he was sent as a medic to the front, and then their daughter died while his wife fled from the bombs, and then two other children died, and those three were blonde like my older Aunt Inge, and then my mom came with two others who were dark, and then their mother died, and I came as the descendent of the replacement children, all dark, and that always came up in family stories: the Polish genes. How these flimsy pieces of paper express the intersection of people and raw power. I don't like handing over ID ever. How arbitrary it is that someone could yell at you—and yet that's never happened to me in the US, though the questions of "what are you" happened from when I was little.

The main effect it had on me was to make me extra sensitive to concepts of ethnic purity as bullshit.

I've been called names a few times because people put me into an incorrect ethnicity, though it only ever really scared me in Germany, because though I am ambiguous-white in the US, for some reason in Germany people think I'm Turkish, and that has meant a few threats and once being refused service in a bar with my cousin. Turkish older men look at me with sad smiles as I order falafel, and they can't believe I would trick them and turn my back on my ethnicity which is really not my ethnicity. All this is nothing major, just enough to be educational, a shadow of what people fleeing and trying to emigrate must feel, in fear and danger as a constant, draining, and inescapable barrier. Does everyone feel this way about passports now?

Ivan's social security card is a rectangle of slim weathered paper. I remember carrying him, at a few weeks old, to the Social Security office in Columbus, proving that he was a new person with his birth certificate. Five years later, I went to Social Security in Georgia after the divorce to get my name back, my first last name, the one I shouldn't have given up, though I had my reasons at the time. It's odd to always be carrying around some man's last name. I thought about changing my name back to the furthest female relative I knew in my mother's line, which is either Adam or Kleidzinski, which would be a lot to adjust to. All this comes up in a barely conscious wave as I slide rectangles of pale paper onto the gray laminate counter at the DMV.

A guy in mini braids smiles at us from behind the desk, and he's wearing a kind of long maroon and dark green winter-print sweater. He jokes with someone who works at the next desk while he's checking things off. He asks for various documents, hands back Ivan's report card because it's too old to be used as valid ID, but then I give him my license, which works to prove our residence, then he's scanning things, then he paperclips everything together.

He asks me to step out of the way and has Ivan stand against a bright turquoise background that is set to the side of the counter. There's a camera right there, one at each station. Ivan stands up straight and then he's done. I say something inane about how there used to just be one camera back in olden times. I'm always saying this kind of stuff to Ivan, and now I understand why old people do this. We are stunned that things change, we are trying to tell our kids that things change really quickly, trying to anchor ourselves to the present and to our timelines, trying to sew the present to the past, basting our layers together. I had thought it was because an old person thought this might be interesting to a young person, but it's a more desperate or necessary feeling, a kind of matching game or lesson to complete in order to keep a hold onto the timelines like you're waterskiing in a rush into the future.

"Did I give you back your social security card?" the guy asks. I check and we have it. He laughs. "If you don't have your documents, it's because I forgot. I always do that." I like that he admits that.

"Are people leaving their documents here all the time?"

He nods. "You wouldn't believe how many drivers' licenses get left here. And people don't think to come back here to look for them!"

We laugh and he points at a diagonal across the waiting area filled with chairs to the next place we must go, a desk with a sign that says to wait behind the red line. So we look and scoot back behind the red line.

SOMEONE SAYS "NEXT" SO WE GO UP to the edge of a partition with a counter. A very pale-white balding smiley guy tells Ivan that he's going to first do a vision test by looking into a large black box with eye holes sitting on the counter, and then he will go into a closed area to take the permit test. He gives Ivan an alcohol wipe to clean the eye test thing, and Ivan rips opens the packet and kind of dabs around the black eyepiece with the pad, not sure what he's doing, and he looks at me doubtfully, like *What does this guy mean? Am I doing this right?* and I point to the places where his nose and forehead will touch the black box. Ivan sets the wipe on the wrapper, and then I take the trash.

The guy says he'll take the trash from us, and then tells Ivan he's got to give me his phone and earbuds because "We don't want no cheetahs!"

And then the guy holds up a hard plastic cheetah, a kid's toy, and waggles it in the air, laughing maniacally. I crack up. Omg, he has a cheetah just for this purpose. I can't stop laughing. Ivan and I look at each other—I know, in that moment, that I've raised him to delight in the absurd. Dadaism, surrealism, the ridiculous as a kind of oxygen, that I can pass on. DMV genius.

Ivan takes the glass egg I bought him this morning in its baggie and puts it in the pocket of his black Adidas track pants. He hands me the flat rounded case for his ear buds and his phone. I tuck them into my bag and he looks at me and then at the black rectangular box that he's never seen before. Of course: as always, this is parenting, the awareness of what you take for granted.

"You just look into those holes, and when you press the metal part with your forehead, something in there will light up," says the guy behind the counter. "Then you read what you see."

I go into the bathroom. I come out and Ivan is gone behind a partition with a closed door to take his exam. I sit down and watch a mom and a girl in the row ahead of me, both with top-knots, one blonde, one dark. The girl says to her mom that they're supposed to go sit over by booth 13, but the mom says no, that's not right. Then later a DMV employee comes out and calls the girl's name and tells her they're supposed to go sit by 13.

I check email on my phone and read that a regional coalition is offering trainings about the crisis of immigrant detention. I had signed up to do civil disobedience training with them before I signed up for the XR protest training, but then family stuff meant I couldn't go. Then in all the buildup about the week with Greta Thunberg arriving in NYC and the climate strike, there was an XR training I could attend, so I went in that direction. I am always checking in with my imagined advice from my dead German grandfather who got written up at work for never joining the Nazi party, for wearing a socialist pin on his lapel to work instead of the swastika, the smallest visible actions and the risk, the mildness of his face and the inner will. I desperately wish I could have met him, but he died of a stroke at sixty-two before I was born, his broken heart and three dead children and then his wife dead when my mother was five. Because of him I think about how even in a narrowed situation you have choices, and you're lucky if some of them involve being able to protest.

Kant and Christ would tell me to go to the immigrant deten-tion protest training, but then that also raises the question of whether I am only doing this so that I can feel not-complicit, a performative thing so I can wave the flag that I got arrested? The larger question of what makes change is much murkier. For

some reason, this mystery emerges each night when I'm wash-
ing pots after dinner, stacking dishes and cups in the dishwasher:
what among the options that I'm not seeing would be the most
effective? Where are the windows I'm missing? I have flicks of
guilt over right-wing acquaintances I've unfriended on Facebook, mostly high school friends from Illinois, because they
started harassing my friends on my timeline. I think in another
version of my life I'd dig into those conversations. But contrary
to popular opinion, people in rural Illinois are not more responsible for Trump than the vast sums of money generated here on
the coasts to support right wing campaigns, the New York and
Connecticut hedge funders who have bankrolled Trump's life.
But on the question of action, I ask myself, how does my job
teaching creative writing put the slightest toothpick in the gears
of doom? The tornado of complicity and resistance goes around
and around with the dishwater down the drain.

AT THE DMV, ANOTHER BOY and his dad go up to the desk,
then a girl and her mom. The kids look so young. I wonder if
each of the parents feels a sense of achievement to have gotten
all the documentation together, always just scraping by with the
forms and the to-do's and the permission slips.

Ivan comes out and he's passed, missed four out of twenty-
five. He's quietly elated—I see relief on his features. My boy,
his light olive skin and smile. He was born with pale pink skin,
dark blue-gray eyes, and blond hair, but his eyes quickly turned
brown, and now he's drifted with adolescence toward the angular southern European darkness of both me and his father. Sweet

boy. Jesus Christ, here I am as in every other minute responsible for a whole other human being.

He holds out his hand and says, "My phone?" and I dig in my bag for his phone and his ear pods in their case with the black cover that he hasn't lost.

We look around, confer about where we are supposed to go.

"What did the guy say?" I ask.

He shrugs and says, "I think he said go back where you were before." I tell Ivan that the other people were told to go by 13, so that's where we go. We look around, and then we laugh about the cheetah guy. I tell him that I love whenever people can make themselves and other people laugh at work, that it's one of the best things there is, because work is long and ridiculous and you have to find fun when you can. I ask him if he could imagine coming to this place to work every day where the customers are always annoyed and stressed. Then we talk about the DMV, how there are no windows and few clocks, how everything is kind of grayish and the lighting is bad, how it seems like you're underwater or in a casino. There's an old snack bar behind us with a popcorn popper, and we talk about how old it is. The whole place looks like the 1990s to me, and Ivan says the striped awning on the snack bar and the decorations are trying to make it look a lot more old-fashioned.

I ask him what kind of questions they asked on his test. He said that some questions were very weird, like "Is the golden rule of driving to get along or get ahead?" I said that that doesn't really seem like a driving question, it seems like a trick, but I guess the right answer is "get along," like Sesame Street. Another question was about how many seconds to wait for a gap before merging, and stupidly specific questions about the dollar amounts of fines and penalties for speeding with a permit.

Near booth 13, a woman ahead of us speaks with an accent that might be Nigerian, and she seems like a grandma. A little girl with a pink headband makes faces at us, and the grandma turns around and asks Ivan how he did and tells him good job. Ivan blushes and says thank you. Then a woman who must be her daughter comes, they gather bags and coats, and the little girl stands near the stretchy rope dividing the seating areas and hangs onto it, twisting her body in a display of frustration, she doesn't want to go home, she says, and yet she's also looking at us shyly with a smile as she whines, and I wave at her and beam the biggest smile I can, and I see Ivan watching me to understand the way I was with him when he was little.

IVAN'S NAME IS CALLED and we go up to the desk of a woman who is all business. She prints a form, he signs it, she takes it, scans it, and she prints another and that's his temporary permit. She explains that the real permit will come in the mail. He looks down, holding the paper by the edges.

"So that's it?" I ask, and she says yes. I pat my bag to make sure my wallet and keys and the folder with all his ID are inside. He smiles, and his eyes relax. As we walk out the door past the podium along the carpet near the old-timey popcorn machine, he says he's so relieved he wants to go home and sleep. His friends Julie and Jacob were worried that he wasn't going to pass because he didn't study.

"You don't want to drive home, do you?" I ask.

"Oh my god, no way," he says, laughing.

We walk out to the gravel parking lot and I am about to open the car door and throw my bag in the back, and he sort of lingers by the front of the car.

Oh gosh, the photo to mark this occasion that I almost forgot!

"Want to take a pic?" I ask. He holds up his permit with his shy smile with the brick DMV in the background and the misty afternoon sky. I text the picture to Cliff, Ivan's dad, Cliff's mom, and my mom at 3:36 p.m.

We get in the car, and I sort of think he's going to fall asleep immediately, as he used to do when he was little after soccer or school.

"I'm getting so old!" he says it like he's sad about it, and we descend into a little cul-de-sac of memory as I pull out of the DMV parking lot, and he says he might just stay living in our house. I say that kids do that sometimes, I never did but my sister did, and the economy today is challenging, especially here on the East Coast, but if you stayed in our basement Cliff's head might explode. Secretly though, I am glad he likes our house, that he doesn't have a need to flee as far and as fast as he can.

He looks at his picture on the temporary permit and squishes up his face, says he doesn't like the picture. I know, I say, every DMV photo of mine I look like a bloated gooney-bird and Cliff looks like an angry supporter of John Brown. It's because they don't tell you they're taking it or the lighting or the angle or something. I think to myself that I've only taken two or three good driver's license pictures. One was my first: sixteen, Joliet, Illinois, barely passed thanks to parallel parking difficulties between snow drifts in January, still growing into my adult face, having lost the baby fat of my cheeks, so I was all nose and eyes and cheekbones, all the Polish darkness, and at the time I hated my face for looking so "ethnic," and I didn't smile in that photo so it looks old-fashioned.

The second good driver's license photo was 21 years later, the day I decided, or knew, that I was leaving Ivan's dad. We were in Georgia, something happened that was just too much. When I am so preoccupied with thoughts of leaving a relationship, when the force of days begins to push me in that direction, I start actually forgetting objects right and left, leaving my house without shoes. During that period of decision I left my thrift-store turquoise wallet somewhere in Walmart. So I had to go get a replacement license at a tiny DMV in a dank wooden shack in Statesboro, Georgia, and the peace in my eyes, the freedom there, the nascent decision and confidence, was caught in that photo. A dear friend, a fellow teacher, had died not long before, and I know it sounds odd, but I felt the dead friend pushing me, almost putting his dead hand on my shoulder, telling me to go, to live while I could. All that was recorded on that driver's license photo. I am dreamy-eyed as if I have just woken up.

WE DRIVE SOUTH THROUGH NEW HAVEN, and on the on-ramp to I-95 we hear the wail of an ambulance behind us. It's too crowded to pull over or stop. I say, "This is an example of something that's confusing even after you've been driving a long time. If you were to pull over, everyone would wreck, so you kind of just try to get out of the way."

We pass the blue and yellow Ikea, which hides behind an odd brutalist concrete building that must have been some civic structure at some point. I always want to go to Ikea, I tell people it's my bar, and now that we live so close, I have driven there a few times when I was agitated and didn't know what else to do with myself. Ikea is like the hope or illusion of order, choosing a colorful towel as a way to brighten your life. Ivan always helps me make design decisions, and I've raised him to be a hawk-eye in the clearance sections.

The highway narrows and lanes merge, a sea of red lights and traffic in the dark, which in German is *Stau,* and it's funny that in both German and English, "jam" means both what you put on toast and the mess we make with cars. I remember learning the word *Stau* in Germany as my cousin Birgit exclaimed it while driving, wondering whether we'd make it to my flight, smell of cigarette smoke in the car, her capable hands on the steering wheel and the way she'd bang it with the ball of her hand and say *Oh mein Gott!*

Because I've just started listening to Spotify, I pull up my meager playlist from my phone on the dashboard holder and turn it on. I keep trying to get Ivan to listen to MIA because at least she's a kind of hip-hop, but he doesn't care much for my girl power, he's already got his AirPods in and he's listening to the bass of sad Latin hip-hop thrumming, and here I am, his mom, sitting next to him, and Santigold comes on, and the album cover where it looks like she's barfing gold glitter, and I say to someone in my past, maybe me, *Well, look, you turned out to be a cool mom with a cool kid.* We tick the exits down, the stretch through Orange and Milford, exit 34, turn through Devon, over the bridge, under the highway, turn to our tiny yellow house.

I park, and Ivan grabs his permit and the glass egg in the Ziploc that he'd placed in the ledge on the dash. We go in and the dog whirls and wags around us, barking, and Ivan brandishes his pieces of paper above her. I drop my bag, shed my coat, and he asks me what part of his permit is okay to post online, and I tell him to cover up the number. I say the pic is okay, but then I don't know, I posted a ballot once and people told me that was illegal. Cliff was running for state house of representatives after collecting signatures in our neighborhood. I have been with Cliff for eleven years and I still don't really understand his political beliefs. I think he thinks mine are weird too. We are both left, we co-exist, but it's unclear which of us is the more pure anarchist. He doesn't believe in political parties, whereas I'm a hardened pragmatist, but we both wish there were more than two parties and that we had a parliament.

I flop on the couch and text my mom the picture of the *Messy* book with a message saying that when I was born, this should have come home with me from the hospital as an owner's manual. A few months later I will find a photo I once took of my bedroom in high school, and it looks like any room I inhabit, including any hotel room almost immediately, with piles of things everywhere: papers, clothes, bits of things to make other things, art supplies, socks, bags, papers, piles and piles of books, cards I mean to write, pens, and computers. It looks like a disaster, but I like process. I like to see things amidst other things, in the potential of becoming.

I text her that everything went fine at court today. She texts back, "I was hoping they would not throw the book at you. I have to get this book now. Trying to get over a sinus/teeth infection, very weird and have to get a tooth pulled. My body is telling me in so many ways that it is revolting, have leg and foot cramps all night long as soon as I relax and feel like a Steh-Auf Maennchen and I get up 7 or 8 times per night."

This takes some explaining. My mom texts like she talks. She doesn't talk with a German accent, but with a very cute emphatic German undertone sometimes in the way she constructs sentences. So she wants to get the book *Messy,* but I tell her I'll just send it to her. Then I ask her for clarification about the connection between her sinuses and her teeth, and it turns out with a little googling that you can get a sinus infection so bad that it goes into the root of your tooth. Or you can get a tooth infection so bad that it runs into your sinuses. The notion of one's head rotting like this gives me the soul shivers. She gets leg cramps, and over Christmas—the last time I will see her before COVID—Cliff and Ivan and I will drive to Illinois and I will buy her the same magnesium powder I drink each night, and it will fix her leg cramps, and I will be so proud. But for now she is a *Steh-auf-Männchen,* a "stand up little man," a German toy that gets up over and over again. Those toys have a rounded weight at the bottom so they always roll upright, the precursor to what Americans know as Weebles. I check the spelling as I'm writing this, and the German Wikipedia entry reads that the toy is connected to the psychological trait of resilience, which I think expresses my mother perfectly, and hopefully me, and hopefully my son.

Sitting on the couch, I peck out a few emails:

Hi K., Your third project can be on anything you'd like to write about! Please bring 3 copies. Thanks! Sonya

Hi all, Remember that for Friday, please bring 3 copies of 500 words toward your third essay project. You can include ideas for the "container" for the essay if you have them. Also we'll be discussing 4 student essays. See you then! Sonya

It's the end of the semester and we're roaring through their essays at breakneck speed. I sit on our gray Ikea couch in a mess of blankets with my laptop and the Ikea plastic laptop desk with a cushion underneath that I bought after I got nerve damage writing that damn book about Hillary Clinton in three weeks, which Cliff warned me not to do, and though it was awful in a lot of ways I learned about my enormous capacity for research. I absorbed and processed Clinton's political career and all of her proposals in less than a month, like the CrossFit of research, which will be the only way I ever understand CrossFit. Then I got this occipital neuralgia, a nerve irritation from looking at a laptop at the wrong angle for that month, so now I periodically have to get nerve blocks shot into the base of my neck.

So that's why I am very careful now to always put my laptop on a lap desk as I sit on the couch. I look at some of the mindless women's sites I need to read at the end of the day as relief from my own thoughts: *Jezebel* (have lost a bunch of good writers lately, taken over by venture capital fuckheads who are ruining it, killed *Deadspin*). *The Cut.* "This Threading Facial Made My Face Feel Like Cashmere." I click on that, it's about a man's hands massaging a woman's face and how that feels good. I don't care about this, but I like reading women's magazines because I like women and I need to read stupid things to turn off my brain. Women seem to yearn for lipstick and dresses and I often feel like I have to fake these desires, I've been very indifferent to the femininity thing, but then again, there's a lot I've learned from women's magazines.

My female friends and I have all helped raise each other. And skincare is women's version of sports, and the writing about women's health is always very important, and *Elle* reviews books, and I like some of the fashion pictures even though they're things I would never wear because I like color and admire women's bodies. For a while, I think in college in the nineties, women's magazines were presented as a demonic plot to induce eating disorders, but I started reading them secretly after college for comfort because I just didn't want to think about politics all the time and had become more and more conscious of everything I missed while immersed in anarchist collectives.

Now I read on *The Cut* that there's a new way to calculate your dog's age in human years but it depends on the breed of dog, and the article includes a very complicated formula that I can't even comprehend; fuck this. "Skin-Care Obsessives Tend to Agree on One Thing," which turns out to be an article about double cleansing, which is I guess cleaning your face twice? I don't know. As a result of reading *The Cut* and having acne on my forehead at age forty-eight I have bought various cleansing potions, Aveda, Trader Joe's oils, and Kiehl's toners.

Somehow I learned in the 1990s, probably from a women's magazine, that Kiehl's was a skincare status symbol in LA. Then I was out there visiting my sister in the early 2000s, right after my ex and I got together, and somehow my sister took me to a party and I ended up drunk in Paul Rudd's bathroom, or the bathroom of a friend of his, before he was famous, and there were sweet little Kiehl's trial sized cleansers lined up near that mirror. The party was not as fancy as it sounds, somehow there was a moment where I could have kissed Paul Rudd, or rather another man asked me if I was available, somehow *for* Paul, and of course being an idiot I said no. But then eventually I was very drunk in the backyard and I found myself pushing cocktail hot dogs into the icing of a birthday cake; was it Paul's? I feel terrible about this swimmy confusing image to this day whenever I see Paul Rudd in a movie.

I have only recently started buying fancy things like Kiehl's moisturizers. I didn't really even wash my face with anything but water until I was maybe in my late twenties. Didn't know how to pluck my eyebrows until I was nearly 30, with resistance to most of the feminine forms of shaping one's appearance because everything was connected via a short bundle of nerves to male attention which was the last thing I wanted, please stop grabbing me and saying gross stuff, please just leave me alone and let me fucking finish my book. Now that I'm almost 50 I am about three times as confident, less traumatized or more therapized and more defended. Jenny taught me how to pluck my eyebrows and then I started using cleansers after I moved to Georgia because I thought I needed to look like a professor so I started to try, mostly from anxiety about being taken seriously so that I wouldn't be manipulated by employers, so that students would take me seriously because my teaching evaluations (and paycheck, job, survival) depended on it. Now look at me, I'm using micellar water and ordering from Glossier and now I even use biodegradable makeup wipes because I am wearing mascara on days I am insecure and need to look like an adult. This is my response to both having a young round face and the soul of a twelve-year-old boy.

Cliff makes dinner, shrimp and frozen veggies and pasta, and as we eat at the table he's explaining a cheating scandal in his class. He shows me pages where he has highlighted all the cheating, which comes from QuizLit.com. Teachers can upload stuff, and all the kids cut and pasted each other's errors. Cliff's voice gets loud because he's irate at his students, and I'm so tired that the volume seems like pinpricks in my ears, which I think is related to the tinnitus.

I eat dinner, then go into the kitchen and wash pots and the skillet from yesterday. I rub a sponge on a solid block of dish soap I ordered online which works really well. I'm very excited about this. I don't know if my sister would like a block of dish soap as a gift, but it brings me a specific daily joy, and I want to spread the word. The satisfaction of rubbing a sponge onto the block, how nice and fine the suds are. How amazing that someone long ago figured out how to make soap from ashes, from lye, from tallow.

I go back onto the couch and open Spotify. I mostly stopped listening to music for eight years, and the easy version of the story is because my son didn't like my twangy alt-rock or my rager girl stuff, but the more complicated version is that for those eight years I was listening solely to Buddhist podcasts and chants to get me through to the next minute. So this fall after Cliff and Ivan wanted to pay for premium Spotify, I decided to make myself an account. And then I searched for a song. I listened to Sebadoh's "Skull" and a whole decade arose. I had to stop the song midway through because the memories were so overwhelming—not bad, just the smells and feeling of rainy Boston, brick sidewalks, cold hands, sniffling, T-Pass, snow. The idea of who I was at twenty-two lives inside that song, autumn in Boston, thrift-store suede coat ripped to tatters, so hopeful and scared, pulling my life together before it very quietly blew up.

When I started to find my old music on Spotify a few weeks ago, I wrote on Twitter that I want to reach back through that song and haul that girl out, the version of me I could suddenly access through the music. I wrote that I would tell that girl that love and compassion don't have to end with you laying your organs on the lawn for another person, that love and revolution don't involve any kind of transcendence at all, especially a transcendence of limits. I wrote that I would take that girl to the edges of things. I would look at the edges of a stone, the outline of a leaf, and say that the edges always shine, the edges are what make a thing beautiful. Taking away someone's edges is destruction. But that will come for her, and I suppose that was the thing she was supposed to learn. That I am still learning.

I put that on Twitter and my friend Tim told me the sentence should appear toward the end of an autobiographical novel, but I don't write novels, though I could claim this was autofiction and change my name to Steve, add a dash of pretend mystery, and then ta-da I'd have a tour de force. Anyway, beneath the tweet about edges is the truth that I stopped listening to music because I felt so guilty for betraying the version of me that lived in each of the songs, the girl who was so alive and jumping and slamming in a sweaty tank top at the shows, pulling a neck muscle with the headbanging, fuck the beer because I'll just spill it, let me dance, bring it, slam into me and I'll slam into you harder, laughing like I am fucking that guitar solo.

Years after I was that free girl at a punk show, I somehow got to the point of lying in a bedroom I didn't want to be in at all, saying "no" first and then "no" second and then being nagged into it, "fucking whatever, just get it over with," to someone who said he loved me for a long time but who was lost on the wrong side of his own face. Being riveted by fear and unpredictability is so easy to confuse with the force of love, and he rang old bells of other hurts, and I thought we were on the same team against those hurts.

Have you ever just closed your eyes during sex, like light as a feather stiff as a board, and willed yourself somewhere else, peeled your soul from your body? I tell myself now that I had no other bargaining chip. I don't know now if that was true. I was frozen within frozen within frozen, turned to salt and stone, and I still carry that version of me wherever I go, a stone totem of silence.

The truth was that I was gathering the force to leave but was not there yet. I am dreamy and slow, and decisions need to gather like thunderstorms. So instead I waited for him to use me and be finished with me because I was more scared of his evil moods and the payback he threatened than I cared about my own comfort. I unsewed my own shadow, like what happened to Peter Pan, and I learned that once you do that, it'll fall back off more easily later, and it never sticks quite the same way again. What I have learned is that if you do that ten times, you get tempted to run into concrete embankments. I had a slab of concrete picked out, a viaduct on the way home from work that seemed to draw my car like a magnet.

There are secrets you keep even from yourself and things you can't say are happening. There are days where you can't bear to list the thoughts you've had, where an account like this would have been far beyond my capacity. So I suppose the ability to narrate a day like this, to allow all the selves to come together in a chorus, is a measure of safety.

And I told myself I had to get through it, and that once I was through, I'd be safe. But then in a shiver I realized that my escape fantasy would leave my young boy without a mother. Between a concrete viaduct and a hard place, I ended up telling someone what was happening, and naming it was a blade that hurt but also cut me free.

I once had the arrogant hope that we might help each other. He, in his chemical haze, broke things in his quest to hold them tight. He wanted a promise from me that I wasn't leaving, and he wanted it bad enough to force it from me. I was deep in my own well so I didn't grab the car keys and leave as I had done many times before, and he had taken to calling it abusive when I would leave to breathe, to drive and sit in some parking lot and cry. Nothing made sense. He knew it was wrong, and he said so later, but he never said the words "I'm sorry." We had so many battles, but most of them were less persistently haunting than this particular transaction.

My amends to myself matters more and it involves seeing that girl, liking her, liking all her sweaty angular messy fervent hilarious chicory cornflower gravel disasters. I was willing to leave and then slowly willing to say what I did. And to stop doing shit like that to her ever again. A fucking hard habit, a big one, soulless and metallic like deep space. I had to write a sign on a piece of paper in permanent marker that said "Don't Keep Secrets" and stick it on my fridge with a magnet for the plumbers and babysitters to see, the first entry in a list of emotional to-do's because I had forgotten how to live. My eternal temptation is to sell out the woman I am and have been, to chloroform her into silence, because I'm scared of the world's hostage situations and she's an easy sacrifice. So this is my amends.

My frozen rage. That is exactly also why I'm such a good girl filled with so much secret shaky ire. It's okay. I have often been fierce, I have done incredible things, but they never come naturally. It always seems like I have to haul the substance to fuel them from somewhere deep in a cavern and then fumble to light them in a rush, barely achieving ignition. In every moment of my life today I doubt my ability to defend myself from myself and others, I doubt my ability to say no, to walk away, to run. The minutes come at me like a flip book of Pantone colors flashing, I'm stunned by them all, they're too fast, and I don't know how adults do it, how they just get through the day saying "That's unacceptable, Henry!" and "Why, I'll give you a piece of my mind" (in a Jimmy Stewart voice). I am both so angry and so afraid.

I FLIP THROUGH SONGS in Spotify, searching, adding my past back together so easily like stringing beads, composing maps to feelings I couldn't feel for a long time. Spotify keeps suggesting newer songs where the women's voices are high and sweet, but I can't really get into that, I like them huskier and low, the alto of Liz Phair and PJ Harvey. I search for Fugazi and there they are, and I smile and add "Waiting Room" and others to a playlist. I search for Public Imagine Limited, the wild-eyed face of Johnny Lydon, thinking about Nicole and Val in high school who wore combat boots, my friend Nicole who I love and am still so close with who got me into PIL and Dead Kennedys, how I adored her, how kind it was that she and her friends rescued me with my weird cardigans and my stammering shyness and my honking laugh.

Cliff asks a question from the kitchen about the rules of driving permits and when and how often Ivan can drive, and I realize that they let us leave the DMV with no instructions. No pam-

phlet, nothing printed. No rules of the road for first-time per-
mittees. I tell him I think we don't have to officially add Ivan to
our insurance until he gets a license, then I google and figure I'll
email our insurance people anyway, but then I can't even remember who we have car insurance with. How alarming. I know it
was GEICO forever, I had GEICO since, Jesus, three fiancés ago.
I've been in a lot of relationships, which is one of those things
that men are allowed to do, but for women it supposedly means
there's something wrong with your soul. Yet there is a part of my
soul that is always separate and alone, a ship on the sea.

Now I don't even know whether we have current insurance
cards. I get these emails, "Your updated policy information" and
I ignore them. I look for it in my inbox and discover that it's
Nationwide (based in Columbus, the blue rectangle logo downtown, where we also get our pet insurance) and then I sign in
(thank god for password managers) and then I print our insurance cards and email our local person about when to add Ivan to
our policy. Then I find and print instructions about the rules for
people with permits.

I look at the driving instruction form. I remember having to
take driver's ed at Lincoln-Way High School in Illinois, sitting in
a room with no windows, then being assigned to go out driving
in the winter on the highways with the football coach. I had acci-
dentally bitten a hole in my cheek so bad that I had put a wad of
toilet paper in my cheek to stop it from stinging and bleeding,
but thankfully he didn't want to talk much, I must have looked
like a nervous rabbit with a wad of chewing tobacco, sweating
profusely and glancing over my shoulder before switching lanes.

The teaching assistant who took over my class today texts me
about the class and about having to diagram a student's essay on

the whiteboard. I have a stab of worry, though I'm sure it went fine. I look at the faces of my students when I enter the classroom each day, each glance a scene in a story, never knowing if I am adding anything to their lives.

I email the teaching assistant back about her final graduate project. I have this impending working-toward-completion feeling at this time in the semester, the overfull scratchy feeling with students, like a storm cloud flashy with lightning, cumulonimbus. The detachment and calm when grades are finally entered. Then the itchy feeling of wanting more students. Thinking about having committed to too much stuff and getting through it. I have been meeting with another student who graduated years ago and is now trying to write about traumatic things that happened to her, and I never know if the advice I'm giving is helpful. It felt helpful. I don't know.

I watch a few episodes of an amazing show, *Mr. Robot,* season 4. I am very attached to Rami Malek and his overbite. Christian Slater has become a dad, though it's a wavering good/evil relationship, and this show ends up being so meaningful to me that the end of it shakes me to the core, no spoilers, but it wrenches up things from my past in a way that few other shows or books have gotten right, and I respect it, and I let it shatter me for a few days afterward. That is what art can do.

Ivan tromps upstairs and says he wants a Hungry Man frozen dinner. Yes, it's true: we feed him a LOT of frozen dinners because there is much—kale soup, salmon salad, assorted pastas and lovely dishes with quinoa—that he will not eat. Fuck it. I was fed out of boxes and bags and instant dinners from the 1970s and 1980s and I'm okay. Well, I'm totally messed up, but anyway I tried, and he has to eat. I cut up lots of fruit for him. I put the black plastic tray in the microwave, and after a few minutes you have to stir the potatoes with one fork, flip the chicken, and then with another fork scoop the brownie into a dish, then let the rest of the dinner cook some more. I put the dinner and milk on the table and then in a few minutes he comes over to the couch with a printed glossy flyer that has his face on it and an order code for school pictures.

"You can still order pictures," he says.

I am momentarily baffled. "But I gave you the form months ago in an envelope with a check!"

"I didn't turn it in."

This is the thing about parenting. You can be a good girl and do all your little forms and then it goes awry anyway. Sometimes he doesn't turn things in. Thankfully he doesn't do this often.

I try to compose my face because this is a pointless thing to be irate about. "It had a check in it. Do you still have the check?"

"I've got it somewhere." He goes through his bag, and the original form with the check is still there, stuffed in the bottom. I rip it up, and then I use the "last chance!" code to order online.

I don't know which package to get. The two-family? His face. Sharp chin, smile. That little face, I remember seeing him in the bassinet and wondering how I gave birth to an elf, and my dear friend Kathy came over and peered in and said he was eerily perfect. I think all babies look like that at first, little birds. His yawn, tiny in the huge wind-up chair. How he was himself even then.

I look at his picture like I might fall into it, seeing how his face records time in reverse. This boy I made. The wiliness of his father in him. Black sweatshirt, a jock, the image he uses to navigate high school. I decide against ordering the two-family package because he's flying out for Thanksgiving on Saturday to

Ohio. I text the code and the website to his dad, the same phone number he's had since I met him at the grocery store in Columbus twenty years ago.

This lapse makes me worry about other forms, physicals, the PowerSchool database, his report card. Grades. My anxiety and how I know it's not my issue. Trying to push him without it being a fixation. College—what will happen to him? I have had to learn—after almost breaking a plate when he told me as a seventh grader that he didn't read *The Outsiders* by S. E. Hinton even though it was assigned—that he is not me. School, for him, is important, and he's learning, but it's not oxygen for him like it was for me. I balance along the edge of parenting by saying exactly what I think, making my case, and then stepping back. Ultimately, the relationship, that tenuous bright golden thread, is the most important thing, and shaming him over anything is not worth losing hold of that. No matter what, I always explain why I am angry and we talk about it and never hold it over each other. I can't abide a simmering resentment in my house, and I will never dole it out, and we both know it.

I read a little, then wash my face, take my pills. I google even though it's too late to look at screens about this infection my mom has in her tooth/sinus. I don't like her doctor, he's so nonchalant. I worry for the rest of the night about losing my mom, and that is what I go to bed with, lying on my pillow, thinking about the Twitter thread of grief from this morning from that guy, thinking about sending love out to Illinois in the darkness and knowing there's a huge force there to receive it, versus knowing a version of life where that force would be gone. When my Aunt Rosy died, I felt like a part of her slipped right inside my ribcage. I miss her, but I also have her with me. But with my mom it would be different because my mom's presence is bigger than any imagining of her. Mom. I know that not everyone has a good relationship with their moms. I have fought fiercely with my mom, we are both very fiery people. She is a mystery to me because she is so much like me, and in some ways the answers to my universe are with her. What I love about her is that she always has adventures, she is always doing crazy things like tearing her rotator cuff punching a snow-cone machine (really) or hurting her wrist by playing the slot machines for hours, or forgetting her purse on top of the car and having it run over by a truck on the highway, and yet the way she tells these stories is so funny, and she's so emphatic about everything! You meet her and you have no choice but to love her and she is excited about German sausage! and coffee! and trying a recipe! And her grandkids! And trains! And . . . that's the thing.

One of my Buddhist teachers says that the state of wisdom in Tibetan is called *emaho,* which is roughly translated as "I am amazed," the experience of wonder at each moment of life, not in a simple childish way, but in a large encompassing way with depth at the preciousness of it. I think my mom has that. I aim for that. What it would be like to lose that conversation. I am not sobbing, I am just feeling the cool of a tiny wet spot on the pillow near the edge of my eye in the dark as I face the nightstand I found at a garage sale in Columbus, Ohio, before my son was born, and the silver Ikea lamp on top of the nightstand next to my earplugs in a bowl with my lime-cucumber lip balm and my Al-Anon daily reader telling me to breathe. I think of dark cornfields, my love for my mom going outward to the west and circling Chicago like a plane. The remarkable thing of having come from such a source, and trying to pass that on.

ACKNOWLEDGMENTS

Thank you as always to my family for their support: Mom and Dad, Glenn and Nicole, Jon and Terry and our extended family of Hermans in Portage, PA, and above all to Cliff and Ivan, who make every day an adventure. Thank you, Cliff, for getting my particular pattern of weirdness, enthusiasm, and doom, and for loving me anyway. Thank you to all of my nonfiction teachers: Bill Roorbach, the kind and generous Lee Martin, and the fantastic and much-missed Lee K. Abbott, and to the greater nonfiction community that has continually nurtured my writing, foremost among that group, Dinty W. Moore.

Thank you to Ander Monson, whose experiments in these one-day essays sparked my thinking that this might be possible. Deep gratitude to my nonfiction family across the country, and while I know I'm going to miss people, I need to at least try to name some of you: Jill Christman, Kate Hopper, and all the rest of the folks from our time at Ashland: Robert Root, Bob Cowser, Steve Harvey, as well as William Bradley and Michael Steinberg (may they both rest in peace), and Joe Mackall. Other friends made through joy in nonfiction experimentation: Adriana Páramo, Heather Kirn Lanier, Daisy Hernández, Amy Monticello, Karen Babine, Sarah Einstein, Joey Franklin, Patrick Madden, David Lazar, Kristen Iversen, Hattie Fletcher, Sue William

Silverman, Sejal Shah, and everyone else whose work I admire but who I have forgotten to mention. Thanks to everyone who supported *Pain Woman,* which seems to have been my diving board off into this experiment.

Thank you to Kristen Elias Rowley for taking on this odd book and to everyone at Mad Creek Books and The Ohio State University Press for making it happen, including Tara Cyphers, Samara Rafert, Jessica Melfi, and Juliet Williams. Thank you to the friends who supported me during my year with COVID, when this was written: my girls Emily Orlando, Gwen Alfonso, and Anna Lawrence, and special thanks to Kris Sealey whose texts kept me going, and Yannik Thiem who I look forward to meeting in person. Thank you to my colleagues and friends at Fairfield University, and to Tim Miller for making me laugh and think during those days of hell, and to Mika for support. Boundless gratitude to besties Barbara Tyler, Elizabeth Hilts, and Nalini Jones for hilarity, support, and understanding, and to Nalini and Tim for their comments on this manuscript. Forever friends Nicole Stellon O'Donnell, Sarah Lovelace, Sharad Puri, Jenny Grabmeier, Brooke Davis, Monica Kieser, Laura Shelton, Blue Chevigny, Kathy Bohley: life is easier because I know you're always in my corner. Thank you to the activists whose histories and actions entwine with my own, who taught me by example, and who made me who I am today: firstly, Heina Buschmann, Jason S-W, Mike, Mark P., Brian, Cindy Crabb, Arwen, Liz, Sam, Reg & Simone & Glen, Jenn Sage-Robison, Irene Mulvey and Jocelyn Boryczka, Vanessa Liles, Michelle Haberland, Jen Bee, Caroline and Miladys at Stratford Mutual Aid, everyone at JwJ, Soli, BLM, UCAN, CCO, ADAPT, AWOL, Extinction Rebellion, AAUP, and so many other acronyms, and every disability activist who taught me how to exist in the world. Another world is possible; maybe we head in that direction in loving coalition, with willingness to change and to give up what we know so that we may gain a better future for us all, with love and courage in our hearts.

21st CENTURY ESSAYS
David Lazar and Patrick Madden, Series Editors

This series from Mad Creek Books is a vehicle to discover, publish, and promote some of the most daring, ingenious, and artistic nonfiction. This is the first and only major series that announces its focus on the essay—a genre whose plasticity, timelessness, popularity, and centrality to nonfiction writing make it especially important in the field of nonfiction literature. In addition to publishing the most interesting and innovative books of essays by American writers, the series publishes extraordinary international essayists and reprint works by neglected or forgotten essayists, voices that deserve to be heard, revived, and reprised. The series is a major addition to the possibilities of contemporary literary nonfiction, focusing on that central, frequently chimerical, and invariably supple form: The Essay.

---

*Annual Gournay Prize Winner